I Think My Friend Has PTSD

Melvin Cintron

Dedications and Introduction

To my friend Cindi whom I served

with in the Gulf War as part of our

347th Med Det / MEDEVAC

Family

I Think My Friend has PTSD By Melvin Cintron

One year ago on the 17th day of the 10th month during a given hour a friend took a moment and, in that moment, took her life. And I, without having slept, woke up in a sometimes dark world that was now a little darker, and a little emptier. I know our friend visited the places inside that many of us visit, its actually not a choice. Places where we keep things we have seen, things we have lived, places where other people died and took small pieces of us with them when we weren't watching what we were seeing.   I have visited where she visited, where many still visit. It's where we speak in silence and in the language that is foreign to the protected, those who have never seen through the eyes of someone else's pain. Yes, it's a language we speak in silence for fear of understanding what we are saying. I think my friend heard herself speak when the world that was listening was just not able to hear her silence.

And so, one year ago on the 17th day of the 10th month, during a given hour, our friend Cindi took a moment and, in that moment took her life, and left us in a world that is now somehow a little darker a little emptier were it not for the memory of her beautiful soul. May God's heart be the only inside place you now visit and may the memory of your friendship, your smile, and the inner and outer beauty you showed to all, make our world if somehow just a little brighter, if somehow just just a little less

empty and little more warm for you having been in it and in our lives.

GGGGGGGG>>>>>∧∧∧∧∧∨∨∨∨∨

To those Families who have known a loss due to PTSD. I hope its harsh reality helps you understand and bring you some peace.

Three things to know for the friends and families of those that chose the most mournful and most final of decisions as a solution. Know these three things:

IT'S NOT YOUR FAULT.

IT WASN'T YOUR FAULT.

IT IS NOT YOUR FAULT.

Try to see the signs, but if you don't it wasn't that you didn't see the signs in time. Try to be there, but it wasn't that you weren't there enough.

Try to be there when you can, but it wasn't that you weren't there.

Try to call as often as you can, but it wasn't that you should have called more.

Try to talk whenever you can, but it wasn't that you could or should have talked more.

Find ways to stay in touch, but it wasn't that you should have communicated more.

Try to text often, but it wasn't that you could have sent more texts.

It's not your fault, but it's just that the closer you were, the more it seems you could have, you should have, done.

IT'S NOT YOUR FAULT, IT WASN'T YOUR FAULT, IT IS NOT YOUR FAULT

To all those who can no longer write their demons temporarily away in the pages of their life, or the dark places that now abide in us, and for me and other contributors, in the pages of this book. For the known and unknown 20 friends that will die of suicide today as you read this "average 20 veterans die of suicide everyday". Can you think of 20 things they could be? Just so that todays 20 don't die unknown, unremembered, uncared for I will choose to acknowledge who they were and who tomorrows 20 are;

1. a mother,

2. a father,

3. a brother,

4. a sister,

5. a son,

6. a daughter

7. a cousin.

8. 8 an aunt.

9. an uncle.

10.   a wife.

11. a husband.

12. a friend.

13. a co-worker.

14. 14 a quite person

15. a very funny person

16. a person that cared

17. a person that mattered

18.   a person I thought I knew

19.a person I wish I had known

20.   person I hope to help before.....

Intro: About Writing this book

I wrote the dedication of this book (to Cindi Concha) over ten years ago as a promise to myself to finish this book for Cindi and for all that still face struggles including myself. Over ten years later I'm still trying to get this book out, so here it is.

When I started writing this book I would tell people what I was doing in many would begin to tell me there struggle or their story and I thought about writing it and including in my book as I requested the permission to do so well they all agree that I could do that I decided that each one of our stories carries a very different weight for each one of us that tells it and no one can tell it the way we want it all even if they repeat it verbatim word for word even with the same voice tones. So what I chose to do was ask "are you willing to write that so that I can put it in the book" and I made a space for each contributor to tell a small but important part of their story as they saw fit. And I thank them and hope they would connect with me for name credit of their invaluable support and the courage to help with their opening themselves up in hopes of helping others that may identify with similar experiences. This is why you will see different writing style and maybe their story, like my story, will help someone else that suffers through some form of PTSD.

In writing this book I found that there is no exclusivity for PTSDS not necessarily a soldier not necessarily a man or a woman but anybody that has demons or dark places that they struggle with and who are looking if not for help at least a reprieve of that struggle even if temporarily. I chose not to list all who are doing so much to help so many of us in our daily struggles from artists to organizations to individuals 2 family members and everything in between for me my biggest strength has been my spirituality in my family who unknowingly helps me cope and feel blessed each and every day of my life.

Although I chose not to list them here, they are available. I hope that you seek them out through talking to a friend to whatever it is that will help you that you seek that out there are tremendous amounts of things to help us even phone apps (I myself use an app that helps me). I plea with you to find your inner support, accept outer help, choose a life, choose to live, yes in spite of the fact we are a little unwell a little to often a little to lost and sometimes a little is to much. Don't be the next statistic and don't let someone else be it either. We are all for each other and sometimes each other is all we can be it's all we need to be to get past the dark visit.

Before you start reading the Book...

First, I apologize here an now so that you don't waste your time reading what the inside of PTSD looks like for so, so, so many and think this can be easily corrected. So my apology is that this book is full of grammatical errors, it is full of incomplete sentences, comas where they don't belong, periods that should be there and periods that shouldn't, sentences that are to long, It's is full of scrambled thoughts with shhtuff that, that I guess is representative of what's in us now. I won't correct it, I wont correct it because It's was a danm hard write for me and for those who shed tears and parts of themselves to give me there stories provided in here and in their own words, and besides being a danm hard to write it's an even danm harder re-read, and there is no way I'm going through it again to make it perfect, we are now so far from perfect and so near to broken so often, that sometimes broken is all that all we can seem to be specially when no one is looking at us or looking but we don't let then notice.

We lost that opportunity for perfect when we realized that no one can give us back the innocence nor the ignorance, that was the us, the us that live within what we were before we were what we are now, before we were this. Yes, this book is a hard read, I wrote it in hopes of helping someone reading just enough to know, we are not always broken and when we are we are not broken alone, and most importantly we are not broken always. Its just that sometimes we are as the Matchbox 20 says "just a little unwell". And for us to acknowledge, and for others to know, that we now live with, and have, dark places inside of us that we have to acknowledge and that have to visit. Help us minimize those dark places, when we visit those dark places, help us not stay in those dark places to long. Help us come back, help us not be part of the suicide statistic.

Sometimes I think life is so much like my friend`s PTSD.

You see, I Think My Friend Has PTSD and like life we just live it as if we are living as if we know what we are doing and as if its ok. So even though I don't want to write this book, I've carried it in me so long, I owe to my friend I think he deserves this, she deserves this, they deserve this. They, we deserve help. She I know another one of my friends also PTSD and I promised myself that I would finish this for her. So here it goes...........

We carried dead, wounded, mutilated, men woman and children of all ages and during it all we ate slept and lived with fear, joy, anger, anguish and every possible emotion in-between and even the in-between of the in-betweens but the bottom line was that we had to continue with life because the fact was that we were on a mission so all these things became normal in as far as this is just part of what we are here to do and so we go along doing it. Normally it isn't until we come back and after the nice pictures of warm reunions tears of joy from those that have no idea of the tears we bring those tears that are made incognito by our smile and initial joy of a return now are no longer in that environment that we truly begin to see what we saw, what we did or did not do, to recognize what was in our path what we lost that we didn't want to lose what we gained that did not want to gain and vice versa. It is the false calm of this return that we realize the gravity of that return, what tears we swallowed, what laughter drowned us, what friends became our life's and what lives were taken from friends and everything in-between.

We carry illness, assault, abuse, trauma, loneliness, despair and desperation, as men women and sadly even as children. During it all we eat, sleep and live with fear, joy, anger, anguish, shame, sorrow, fear, loneliness, and every possible emotion in-between. The bottom line was that we were on a un-routed journey where all these things seen to become normal in as far as this is just part of the life what we are here to live and so we go along doing it. Normally it isn't until we, and only we, in hidden rooms where

no one can here do we whisper the name of the
darkness that visits us as we attempt to give color to
the expectation of normalcy, before someone can
hear the stories we whisper to ourselves in those
silent rooms. That place where we truly begin to see
what we carry, scars hidden behind smiles, smiles
that themselves have scars that need no further
make up, frowns that we attribute to other things
not known as reality. Here also, we hear what we did
or what was done to us, what we did not do, or what
we let be done, to recognize what was in our path
what we lost that we didn't want to lose what we
gained that we did not want to gain and vice versa.
It is for so many of us, only in these rooms that we
exist within the solitude, albeit it amongst a

multitude of multitudes, that we realize the gravity of what many return to without ever really having left it. And so they too know the taste of what tears we swallowed, what laughter drowned within us. What words we never pronounce, what friends became our life's desire for normalcy but not our reality, and what lives were taken from us. The lives we could have been living, the ones we may still live if only, if only it weren't for........

So, some lives are made of such moments some more drastic than others but depending on the focus of, what is perceived or even fact, not what is seen or lived but carried by who is perceiving what has been seen or lived, since perception is real to the perceiver.

These are, and this is, the true stories as seen through the reality of we who now live with what with the contradiction of reality we abnormaly perceive as our normal.

I think my friend has PTSD. Sometimes my friend smiles too much, oftentimes my friend seldom smiles at all. I think my friend might have seen too much and now can't un-see what has been seen. My friend can't seem to forget the things that are now remembered and are unwillingly kept as reminders of things we thought we'd forget. Maybe things will be better for when my friend goes back home, but I think my friend is also worried about going home like this, or taking these kinds of things home. But I don't even know what "these things" are. I wonder if my friend even knows or would answer if I asked. I really like my friend and want to help, but I don't know that I even know how to help. I'm trying to be careful, I don't want to lose my friend since sometimes I don't know that we're really that close although sometimes I think that we are. I don't want my friend to think I'm saying, "Hey, you got a problem." I mean, what if my friend really doesn't and I'm just noticing things that aren't really there? Maybe it's just all the stuff going on now and it will probably be okay if I leave it alone and accept my friend as a little changed, a little different.

Maybe my friend just needs to get home and put this in the past. That should be easy to do, shouldn't it? I mean, it's just memories, it's just things we've seen, things we've done, things we felt and things we didn't let ourselves feel. Maybe the fact that my friend has been through these types of challenges before, I think, means that my friend learned to deal with this, be able to handle it and be able to man up or woman up, however the saying goes. Maybe my friend's family will be able to help. As I remember, my friend used to enjoy family time a lot. My friend speaks of them highly and often. Yeah, I think my friend's family should be able to help if there is any help to be done. Shouldn't they? Yeah, maybe getting back to family will help – how can it not? Family always understands, don't they? Maybe seeing other friends will also help. Maybe getting back to the normal routines, maybe just being away from these things. Shit, that's a lot of maybes and now I'm back to my original concern. I think my friend has PTSD.

I've been wondering how to approach my friend about the issue regarding the possibility of my friend having PTSD. I mean, how do I approach it? I mean, do I just walk about and ask my fiend to talk about what's going on, about seeing things that are maybe not there to be seen? Do I ask my friend to talk to someone else? Maybe a chaplain. Maybe a family member. Is my friend going to perceive this as me insinuating that there's a problem, that maybe my friend is weak? I wonder if my friend feels that there is really no one to talk to about this. Or maybe my friend has already talked to someone else. I mean, who am I to think I'm the only one my friend can talk to? Damn, I always thought myself pretty good and smart, but I'm actually feeling kind of stupid. I wish I could understand what's happening a little better, but every damn thing seems to move so fast and every damn thing seems to move so damn slow. Why are so many cuss words popping into my head? I don't even want to be politically correct, but I'm thinking there is no pretty way to say these things. There are no pretty words to cover up the fact that I think my friend has PTSD. There are no beautiful words to say it with. Actually I hope there never are any beautiful words to say it with because for my friend I think this may be an ugly reality.

I bet whomever my friend has talked to it has probably been more or less superficial talk. Maybe my friend even talked about some of the "stuff" my friend has seen or been through or done. Perhaps my friend saw some wonderment in the looks of those listening as my friend talked. Who knows, maybe even some amazement, shock, or awe as my friend attempted to relate stories, anecdotes, or just plain old "stuff". Maybe in the midst of talking to others and even family my friend also saw things in their eyes, all those things and more, except that maybe, maybe what my friend didn't see in their eyes was actual "understanding" or actually comprehending what my friend was saying and more importantly, what my friend was not saying.

Maybe the more my friend talked with family, the more my friend talked with friends, maybe the more my friend talked, the more my friend thought it was better not to talk much.

Maybe it's better, yeah, maybe it's better to not talk to eyes that become stares, stares that become empty looks, empty looks that cannot be filled with what my friend was trying to show them. Yeah, it must have been superficial because I still think that my friend has a PTSD problem. I'm almost sure that with all my friend saw in everyone's eyes, my friend didn't see in their eyes what my friend was seeing, what my friend was feeling. Yes, I'm sure they were listening, they were hearing, but I don't think my friend saw understanding. Who knows, maybe my friend even thought, wow, which one of us is it that has the thousand mile stare? But then again I'm sure my friend understood that the family, family members can love, can listen, can sympathize, can think they understand, but how could they? I mean, really, how could they really understand? There's no way for them to see through my friend's eyes, to feel through my friend's heart, but how could they, they were not there, they did not experience what my friend experienced. They can love forever, they can care forever, they can want to help forever, but to really understand, understand in their protected world? Maybe never.

The other day I saw an acquaintance, ok I'll call her a friend too. She said she would deal with some stuff when she gets home and that she was fine (I approached her as practice to approaching my friend). I guess talking to her maybe was practice for how to or how not to talk to my friend whom I think has PTSD. Anyway I was talking to her about "things" and "stuff" and what I thought it wasn't really about her, it was about me thinking that my friend has PTSD. Anyway after that and after she had been back home a few months she sent me some text messages saying she wanted to go home and I'm thinking what a crazy ass chick, you were just home and indicated that it was good to be back home, but it wasn't the same "being back home".

She wanted to move on to another place or just move on, and I thought man if she had a PTSD problem she'd be in trouble. She was texting me how things didn't seem to make that much sense, how things seemed somewhat different, especially people running around like everything is so important and she was trying to make sense of how those important things didn't really seem that important. How they seemed the same and how they seem so different now. I texted back trying to pin down what the actual issue or problem was, but it seemed to come down to "stuff" and "things" that she was going through. And so I thought, yeah, that's a little adjustment to go through, but at least she doesn't have to worry about the fact of the things that my friend is having to deal with because I really think that my friend might have PTSD.

Because of this, I can't really worry about my other friend for now. She's fine, isn't she? To add to complicate about the last visit to her sister's place and how this time it was so different. My friend had been in a "situation" in Afghanistan that she told me about and she indicated that she went back home but she didn't feel comfortable going to all the crowded places that she and her sister would go to in the past and would enjoy deeply. In fact, she said that she felt very lonely, even with all those people, even with all those people around her. She said they took a trip as they normally did to look at the changing of the colors of the leaves as she had always loved. She loved how rich and vivid he colors always seemed to her.

Then she kind of looked at me and said that this time she still saw the colors, but somehow they didn't seem as vivid or as alive anymore. They just seemed like colors, they just seemed like leaves, leaves, leaves changing colors, nothing more. She talked about waking up at night, more frequently than she could remember and not knowing why. She talked about being anxious in all kinds of situations and even being anxious about being anxious. What the hell does that mean, I thought? I again wondered, what am I supposed to do with that? Why are these people telling me those things? I mean, what the hell is going on with all these people? I mean, I care, I want to listen to all their regular stuff and their little stories and all that, but

I mean, they're okay. They don't have a problem, do they? It's almost like they don't see the real problem of what I'm trying to deal with in wanting to understand and see how I can help my friend. I mean, don't they see that I'm concerned about my friend and the fact that I think my friend has PTSD.

As I said, I think my friend has a PTSD problem and I'm trying to figure how to approach it, how to reach out and maybe even how to help my friend without causing issues between us. The problem is, that in the middle of all this I keep getting interrupted by all these different people that are distracting me from being able to deal with how to help my friend because I think my friend needs help. For example, I'm minding my own business and my own dilemma, and this other friend I have starts talking to me and relating their stuff and jus starts telling me all this shit that I guess they felt they need to tell at least once so that it doesn't died inside them everyday I guess, who the hell knows, but Like I said I really dont see why they cant see that the real problem is that I think my friend has PTSD and Im trying to figure out what to do about it. So, again, I'm minding my own business and my own dilemma, and this other friend I have starts talking to me and relating o heir stuff an incident and "stuff" that happened to him. I think he started sharing because he saw my concern for my friend and thought that it might help me understand what my other friend was going through. I thought, how the heck does your stuff relate to my friend? It seems more like an issue of relating to your kids, but nonetheless he proceeded to relate to me an experience that I guess he thought was pertinent.

He said, you know in one of my tours I witnessed so much civilian suffering, especially with children. He said that while he was witnessing these things as part of his missions, he really did not have a problem doing the mission because it was just that, plain and simple, a mission. But somehow, when he got home and was no longer in "mission mode" there was something unsettling about those missions now that he had time to unwantedly reflect on the things that he had done or he had seen or even that he had not been able to do. He said that one of the first times that it really hit him was going to church one Sunday after being home for a while. He said he and his wife and kids went to church like they sometimes did one Sunday morning. He was walking behind his wife and as she entered the church with both of their young children following behind her he noted that the kids, walking in, behind her and in front of him, he noticed how they were well-dressed, how they were well-fed, how protected from the things that he had seen and the places that he had been than they were. Yes, he noted, he noted them needing nor wanting for anything. As the kids walked in the church door it wasn't that he froze, it wasn't that he just stopped, it was that he could no longer move or even knew if he could move. At that moment the memory of every child that he had seen and physical states that he choose not to share all of a sudden flashed before his mind's eye. The emotions seemed to parade in slow motion across his soul as they entered his memories at the speed of light. He said that within the eternity of fifteen seconds he thinks he really did find himself unable to move, unable to find himself. In the end he ended up not walking in, but rather sitting in the rectory building next door waiting. He said sometimes he feels he is still sitting there, still waiting, not knowing why or what for, but still waiting. He said his wife asked him to keep a diary for their young children during the time he was serving. He said that now he doesn't really know if he wants them reading it, since he's never really

being able to get though reading it all since writing

it. while serving in his first conflict. Then he shared

this portion of that diary:

Dear Hardy

it's 23 March 1pm yesterday turned
out to be a pretty horrible day
with nothing pretty about it we
did about 4 missions yesterday with
full loads each time and with
small children and women in each
load it was like a nightmare,
at about 8pm we had a mass
casualty situation it seems that
the Republican Guard decided to
wipe out a town where alot
of the resistance fighters lived
they shelled the town with
mortars and artillery to destroy
as much of it as they could then
they went in and stationed them-
selfs on top of the houses and
began shooting all the women
and children and babies and
whoever else was around, we were
getting casualties faster then we
could handle them, God it seems
so unbeleivable, crying children
full of shrapnell and gunshots,

Mothers crying looking for their
children knowing that they where
probably dead, and dying babies
laying on the stretchers as we
tried to keep them alive and
wandering how the hell could anyone could just shoot all those
women and small children, it made
me so furious and so sad I dont
even remember seing movies that
where as horrible as This reality
or Maybe its that being part of
this reality makes it more horrible
the last load I took I had a
teenage boy and a teenage girl both
with gunshot wounds and in one
of the Litters I had 2 small children
one was about 2yrs old and the other
about 5yrs old the 2yrs old had a
gun shot wound in the abdomen
his heart stopped when we had him
in the E.R. (Emegency Room) but we
got him goin again he had big
Round eyes and he wouldnt close
them he had tears in them and

just seem to stare at me I held
his hand as the other medics put
a "y"tube in him so that we could
keep an oxygen tube inside his
mouth and pump oxygen into him
with an ambu bag during the one
hour flight, the other kid had
alot of shrapnell wounds and
he was calm during the flight
unfortunately the 2yr old died
on us about 15 minutes before we
landed we kept the oxygen on him
till the evac hospital took him they
tried to revive him but he was to
far gone, damn I really thought
he would make it, he felt so strong
when I was holding his hand but
we are not god so I guess we
cant save them all, It hurts when
you loose them though specially, if
you think about it and let it get
to you I'm trying not to do any
of that right now, its just missions
that we have to do, for now
thats all that this can be

just missions, when I get home I'll take a day or two to reflect on all of this and cry or do whatever comes at the time, but for now its just missions that daddy has to do before he gets to go home.

I love you my children and I miss you very much, I'm very tired, we didnt stop till about 2AM last night and naturally the weather was horrible it was very cold and it rained all night with strong winds plus the aircraft needed maintenance so we ended up staying at Charlie instead of flying back to Romeo our tents where already taken down so I had to sleep inside the aircraft on a litter it wasnt much of a sleep the wind kept rocking the helicopter and it was cold as heck and everything is muddy as can be, oh well I'll try to get some peaceful rest soon I need it
Love Daddy

As I finished reading it I looked at him and felt like, ok, what the hell am I supposed to say to that? I thought wow, that's a heck of a thing to happen to someone and that his incident was interesting and I hoped that he had a way to deal with that, but I really didn't see how that would help me with the issue of helping my friend and the remaining fact that I think my friend has PTSD. I mean this guy's issue was something he could talk to me about, so I don't think that he had that much of a problem, did he? I mean it's some horrible "stuff" no doubt but hey, the guy was lucky enough to write it all down and get it out of his system right?. Like I said, when I finished reading that I felt like, ok, thank God that's over for him and that he is no longer dealing with that, so he no longer has a problem, but I didn't really say anything because he looked at me and started talking before I could say anything. He said you know, while I was in the midst of it I convinced myself that it was just a mission and it really was, just another mission. At least it is, or it was, when you're in the middle of it but somehow, somehow when you are no longer in the environment when there are no mortars to worry about, when there is no external enemy or threat to occupy your thoughts, when being aware of your surroundings no longer means that you are the surrounding, when the adrenaline lays dormant as a sleeping dog waiting to have its growl wake you in your restless sleep somewhere between your nightmares and your realities as you stand sweating memories that others will never remember like tear that dry inside you as if almost to deny you relieve as they drown you in the humanity of who you were before you were what you are now whatever the hell that now is, whatever in heaven you wish it could be, it should be. The you before this you.

The you before this you!? Who the heck can make out what that's supposed to mean, was he messing with my head or what. Anyway he was starting to distract me from the real issue of me trying to figure out how I can help my friend because I think my friend has PTSD.

I was at a get-together the other day and another acquaintance, ok a new friend, sat next to me and I told him that I thought I had a friend that may have PTSD and that I was wondering about it. He said that although he had been in the military and had experienced a few things. He spent a lot of time in Iraq and Afghanistan, but he was also a Special Agent with the Air Force Office of Investigations (AFOSI) and a routinely worked a lot of crime scenes and homicides. He felt that his involvement, or job, as an intelligence and special investigator was really something that changed him in his way of seeing and relating to life, to others, to "things". I thought ok I'm telling this guy about PTSD related issue and he wants to talk about things that didn't happen in combat. So

I'm thinking really? You think I got time for listening to non-PTSD problems or issues? But I really liked and enjoyed his company so I listened. He told me of pretty graphic things that he had seen and continues to see and to have to investigate. He said it was mainly dealing with fellow soldiers who end up taking the path of despair, to the point of taking their lives or just giving up and destroying their lives. He kept telling me about some of his experience whereby he had to view autopsies as part of his job or investigations. And sometimes it was seeing soldiers that had committed suicide. It was kind of weird because it seemed like he was talking to me in somebody's voice in seeing the reality of a troubled person who blows a bullet through their head and crazy stuff like that, or having to break the curled up fingers of a burnt soldier to try and get fingerprints. He has told me about situations where he has dealt with lots of dead bodies and aggravated assault cases. Before this he said he was always optimistic and smiling; he always greeted everyone with a smile and hello. Now he's still pleasant, but he doesn't have the same happy smile and gleam in his eyes. He said he no longer looked at life the same way; life...it's so fleeting and you'll never know who's going to be next on the slab. It could be the guard working at the front gate or the girl working behind the counter in the finance office. He doesn't smile like he used to.

I asked my friend about some of the things he's seen and he told me about a case he had while working at Keesler AFB, MS. A two year found wondering around a trailer park only wearing a pamper said his mother left with his father; an active duty Air Force (AF) technical sergeant. The mom who was also an AF technical sergeant and the estranged wife of the father never returned. When questioned, the sergeant claimed he hadn't seen her. The AFOSI agents at the detachment dove into a relentless search for the wife exhausting all measures and even reading the husbands mental health records. In his records he described a location in the Desoto National Forest he referred to as his "favorite place". He once told his therapist he thought about committing suicide in his favorite place. He even went as far as detailing how long it took to drive there and the dirt road leading into the forest and the foot path leading to the exact spot. After three days of searching, two agents found a piece of corrugated tin over a fresh mound of dirt in the Desoto National Forest. After inserting a stick to check for its density (it went straight down) the agents radioed back that they found what they thought was the grave. This is where my friends said he parts came in; he was one of the agents responsible for actually unearthing the body in the grave. He said the closer they got to the body the stronger the putrid odor became. Some of the more experienced agents and law enforcements officials became to take bets on which the neophyte sheriff deputies would punk first. The smell became so intense some of the younger cops began running into the woods to puke; all the while my friend said he was still removing dirt. He said as they got closer to the body they began to use their hands and once they started seeing long strands of blond hair they switched to removing the dirt by using paint brushes. He gently swept dirt from the body only to be shocked by one of the most horrific sights he's ever seen. The face appeared under a veil layer of dirt... the skin was jet black and the eyes where jutting out of their sockets and the tongue was fully extended between the lips. He said the crazy thing about the color of the skin on the face was she was a very fair Caucasian female and the skin on the rest of the body was a normal complexion. They delicately removed her body from the grave and set her on a body bag next to the grave. The grave was over five feet deep and they continued to comb the dirt in the bottom of the grave looking for evidence; my friend said when he looked up he was looking directly eye level of the corpse and could visually see her flesh changing color as it was exposed to hot humid Mississippi night. He said at the time that really freaked him out but he couldn't say anything. After they finished at the grave he transported the body back to the forensic pathologist morgue and conducted a forensic autopsy on her body. They finished at 0500 and at 0700 before he could get in bed he was called by the office and told the husband had committed suicide and he was needed on the scene. When he arrived he discovered the husband had indeed committed suicide by sucking on the business end of a 12 gauge shotgun. The entire top of his head was missing with the exception of one eye still intact. He said wall behind his body was covered in blood and brains and when he looked at the body, he could see straight down the sergeant's throat from the open skull that was once a head. Another 12 hours on the crime scene and autopsy before he was able to get to bed. But he wouldn't have PTSD from that would he? That's not the same as being in combat and seeing your buddies shot and blown up in front of you is it? Well anyway he said he had at least 18 more stories like that, but he wouldn't have PTSD from that would he? I mean did he even know those people, I don't think that's the same is it? Either way he says he spends a lot of time doing fitness activities (weight training, running and cycling) and reading to alleviate the stress brought on by the constant memories that come to him in his sleep. It works most of the time but the memories still seep through the cracks of the façade he builds to keep them out. He said he's aware of the fact that he no longer developments social bonds like he use to and he's working on that too. He laughed about the conversation he had with a VA psychiatrist that told him his issues were normal for what he's been through...normal? How do you fix normal? Well I'm sure he'll work it out?

He indicated that he gathers with family and friends as often as he can, but that even in their midst, surrounded by family he trust and loves he felt disconnected. I was surprised to see a certain level of emptiness in his voice or maybe his eyes or maybe, maybe just an emptiness in him. Then again maybe it was just something that I was noticing that really wasn't there, who the hell knows what if anything was missing in his look, in his eyes. This is the mistake I don't want to make with my friend. I wondered if I looked more closely at my friend would I see that same emptiness. But then again I thought, how would this guy I'm talking to who feels disconnected when he's with friends, has a distant stare, doesn't sleep well, as he told me, relate to my friend whom I think has PTSD. How can he relate since he doesn't have PTSD, does he? Because for sure I think my friend does and their situations are totally different. So it's not the same, is it? He told me more of that kind of "stuff" and I thought that this may be similar to what my friend might have been exposed to, but maybe not – I wasn't always there. And besides, it may be similar but it was not the same. I mean, hell, this guy was operating and working normally and still doing a job. I don't see that he has an issue, or would have, so I need to just stay concentrated on the issue at hand that is that I think my friend has PTSD.

Of course its not easy cause everywhere I turn

someone is sharing their experience but how is that possible there cant be that many people who might be like my friend might be, can there? Anyway I recently heard from a friend about her sister and similarities and concern she shared that just like I was concerned about my friend she was concerned about her sister so I contacted her because I wanted to prove that the only real problem was that I think my friend had PTSD everyone else is ok. How can people not und understand that the problem is that I think my friend has PTSD!. Anyway her sister shared that---------------- I took my oath to "support and defend the Constitution of the United States against all enemies, foreign and domestic; that I would bear true faith and allegiance to the same" very seriously. The U.S.'s long history in Afghanistan, spurred on by political decisions at home and abroad, and explained by state-sponsored stories that captured the imaginations, irritations, and angry soul-fire of men drove the U.S. to embark on a 'reconstruction and stabilization' mission in the mid-2000's. That mission was something with which I was determined to help in my role as a diplomat. The men and women I served with – from numerous U.S. agencies, the U.S. and other countries' militaries, international organizations, and the local Afghans gave so much – more than any really had to give. Over the days, weeks, and months there, I spent every waking moment either doing or thinking about doing something—whether on my own or as part of a team to 'solve' the myriad of problems there. I gave political, economic, and governance advice; developed strategic plans; made personnel decisions; provided resourcing recommendations; and worked to shape and implement governance and economic improvement efforts. In doing so - I experienced impossible decisions of where to deploy insufficient resources, an inability to effectively address abject poverty, pain, and drivers of instability, and felt the despair of the Afghans who were relying on us for help.

We did a dance with wily, sometime corrupt, sometimes simply savvy, local leaders who were themselves trying the thread the needle of peace and prosperity for themselves and their communities while also dealing with overgrown desires for power, wealth, and domination over others – sometimes from others, sometimes within themselves, sometimes both. That dance was supposed to make things better – instead it got people killed, maimed and destroyed -- us and them. Having to decide between bad, horrible, and worse, over and over and over wore me down. And the good I hope we did, and we did do a lot – more than anyone could humanely accomplish without giving up pieces of themselves, felt like a drop in the sea of bad. But in retrospect, long after leaving the war, I came to realize that the human heart—both of the individual and of society—can only take so much before it breaks.

Like a dam that develops hairline cracks and small leaks, it's not always obvious what's broken or how to fix it. Despite our best efforts, the mess I entered and was determined to make better, continued to deteriorate in countless small ways. We poured our very life blood into it—some, everything they had—in an attempt to fix what was in many ways, beyond repair.

As I did this, my mind and spirit began to break down too. My demons came to

rest with me slowly, oh so slowly. I didn't see them taking setting up camp, evicting my higher thoughts, eviscerating my dreams. Each personally known and worked for project that failed, destroyed dream, interlocutor executed, convoy hit, colleagues hurt, child wounded and afraid, livelihood destroyed, family killed, fallen solider -- particularly those I knew personally, and every uninformed and judgmental leader who had no idea what was going on and didn't care to listen or understand -tore at my soul. And the stories the soldiers – some still teenagers – told me over shared meals in the mess hall further broke my soul. After my first tour I didn't want anyone to touch me. For an entire month – I wouldn't even let my family hug me. But, I was 'fine'. I stridently insisted on it, both with myself and others. The only other tip-off that something was wrong was when they asked me go back – I felt relief. I thought that strange – but I realized at least when I was there, I felt alive. To be home felt like torture -- to pretend that regular life mattered. Who cared about daily work and social events, when I could be doing something to try and stop the horror I knew was happening overseas?

Back again in Afghanistan, I again worked 12-18 hours every day, limiting myself to 8 hours on Sunday, if possible. At one point, someone had to get a key to enter my room and shake me awake to see if I was still alive after incoming mortar dropped on base near me. I didn't hear the sirens, I didn't go to the muster point, I didn't hear the phone calls, I didn't hear the knock on my door – I was too exhausted. I kept it at bay for almost two years after finishing my tours there, or at least ignored it. A slow decent into the darkness – so slow I almost didn't know it until I looked up and saw nothing but shadows. And then – a lightening round through despair, terror, and then numbness that stayed – because what other choice did I have? I finally called home one night two years later from another high-threat foreign posting asking my family to stay on the line with me till I fell asleep. I had a plan, a specific plan that would end it all – which I knew wasn't okay. The next morning, I walked myself to into the medical unit at the Embassy. I couldn't talk except to say, "I'm not okay" and just nod 'yes' or 'no'. The doctor sent me to a psychiatrist – who said I had PTSD. That broke my silence – I laughed. I couldn't! I wasn't in the military. No one died in my arms! I couldn't...I couldn't. For years after returning home - I suffered nightmares, waking drenched in sweat —unable to fall back asleep for fear of the terror that awaited me. Flashbacks, a repressed sense of terror, feeling trapped, and abject hopelessness was the subconscious foundation for trying to 'get on with life'. My once amazingly precise and accurate memory turned into unreliable Swiss-cheese. I lost the ability to go to parties, large gatherings, church, and even work meetings without a foundation of anxiety and fighting a rising sense of panic. I no longer could sit with my back to a door, and experienced a racing heart and shaking limbs during fireworks or after a car backfired.

It took me over 10 years to be able to again consistently do my own laundry, shop, cook, and clean for myself – so many things just became impossible. I felt, and still do at times, deserted by my country. Very few seem to know, much less care what you do, what you sacrifice – especially if you don't wear a uniform. That includes many of my family and friends. I can't seem to explain in a way that most people can understand what went wrong – why I felt the way I did, and sometimes still do. I didn't shoot a gun or even carry one. And even if they want to understand – I learned they can't in many ways. It's almost impossible to understand if you haven't been there, and sometimes – even if you have. Truly, war is hell. And every patriotic fireworks program, parade, and military recognition effort makes my soul shrink and feel a little smaller – because a) we're aggrandizing something so horrible, that although perhaps necessary at times, is full of darkness, and b) to the world – my sacrifice isn't worth recognizing despite being there in the same place, swearing the same oath, working and walking side-by-side with the military for the same ends. Which makes me feel really alone, and for some reason I feel guilty too – I shouldn't have PTSD.

Taking a years-long break from my former profession – in addition to the many previous years of very expensive therapy, visits with doctors, and countless yoga, meditation, exercise, writing, and breathing exercises I engaged in just to minimally function within that world, finally gave me time to truly heal. A psychology professor helped set me free to accept 'what is' instead of pining for who I was before PTSD when she said, 'having PTSD is like getting your arm cut off – it won't grow back. The only difference is that no one can see you're missing an arm'. Her framing helped me to move forward with a new normal – being grateful for the things I have and building from there. I now have more good days than bad and am moving forward with life again. However, I started to stutter after

returning home; that, and a hand and arm that shake when I'm emotional (which I can usually hid from most people) – still remain as observable artifacts of that time. For a long time during this 'decent' that no one could see, me included, I sought to project perfection thinking it would provide protection.

"The Beast Inside"

Perfect skin

Not even a flaw

Placid expression...

Deception.

Beast's sharp claws

Run thru my memories

Shredding soul -

My enemy.

Flayed and frayed

A spirit confined

Wrapped 'round brittle rod

Distorted mind.

All the while

I turn a blind eye

Ignoring --

The beast inside.

And now – I simply seek for progress each day, try

not let the darkness 'drive',

and to

love as much and as many as I can, and let go of the

outcomes. Darkness Driving??

Oh – the darkness

It's set up camp.

I Think My Friend has PTSD By Melvin Cintron

More of a well-established settlement

In my mind,

With satellites in My heart

And my soul.

We wave hi most mornings. Its

inhabitants are needy,

But we've grown accustomed to

Living together -

For many years now.

They're often saying something,

Sometimes a yell, sometimes an insistent whisper -

-

"You're terrible" "no one loves you"

"Just let go of the steering wheel"

"You're so alone"

But I know now —

Those residents are just suffering from

Hurts, bumps, and bruises

In truth — some deeply traumatic

events And they're sharing their hurt

with me In hopes of not being so alone

So I try to love them too, While not letting them

drive This car,

This life, This heart, Or this soul

Totally into the dark.

Afghanistan was the proverbial straw that broke the camel's back -- my mental health. I've served in other places, with other people, and faced stressors that are hard to describe, much less fully comprehend. Most of my colleagues came out okay

-- at least, I think so. I actually don't know, because we don't talk about it.

I'm angry that we don't. Instead, we tell each other things like, "Some people just aren't cut out to be diplomats." That attitude still angers me. I don't dare share with the military units I served with; I don't want to add to their burden. And

since we don't talk about it in my former profession, I feel like I don't belong, that

I'm not allowed to be broken. And I worry how many others are broken, too.

So, after reading this, that she shared, I thought yeah ok but she's glossed over the whole problem, didn't she understand that I think my friend has PTSD? How can anyone miss that, that's the real issue and I need to see how I can find out and, if so, how can I help my friend. Is it that people just don't get it? I really do think my friend has PTSD!, and what am I going to do if he does???!

Well I cant seem to get away form people telling me things that miss the point that's important, whats important is that I think my friend has PTSD, and yet here I met someone that recounted this to me and something he read on a desk in Iraq,

:::

"Life should not be a journey to the grave with the intention of arriving safely in a pretty and well preserved body, but rather to skid in broadside in a cloud of smoke, thoroughly used up, totally worn out, and loudly proclaiming "Wow! What a Ride!" (Hunter S. Thompson)

This quote, posted on a dusty desk in Iraq as a 20-

something year old sergeant on my first combat tour always seemed to stick with me. At the time, it was very inspirational and spoke to how I felt. I was...invincible, ready to do what I was there to do – the first time, the second time, and every other time.

Before I arrived to Iraq on my first deployment I had been part of many meetings and leadership gatherings talking about Soldiers with "problems" from previous deployments and those likely to have this "problem" based on surveys and command experiences. The tone of said conversations was always a combination of pity and disgust. A Soldier who was bothered enough by experiences in combat to ask for help was not and still today, is not widely accepted. I was part of the problem as I too believed that PTSD was a matter of self-control and not an ailment or an injury. During my first deployment, as young and inexperienced Sergeant I saw first-hand the horrors of combat just like every other Soldier that was with me at the time. I saw many being immediately affected emotionally, physically, and spiritually, however, I dove into the work of being a leader, a planner and an accountable individual to give my thoughts little attention.

That first deployment of a year seemed to go by rather fast. I felt unaffected and effectively forgot or just didn't think about the experiences of combat as I dedicated myself to the daily routine and the responsibilities that I had to those working for me. At times, I would recall an unpleasant experience, such as a roadside attack on one of our many convoys, the difficulty of talking on a radio while under stress, the frustration of not being able to stop a bleeding injury or to comfort a wounded Soldier or even a civilian. I developed some proficiency with the local language and I would unwillingly become a translator, and often, the bearer of bad news to a family. Accidents were common and unfortunately collateral damage resulting in injury or death of innocent bystanders was, for a long time, a common occurrence. – I quickly pushed these thoughts aside as I was always "busy" and there are always better things to think or worry about.

By the end of that first deployment I was a little more

experienced, more confident in my abilities as a Soldier, and a lot more certain that I was simply not one to be negatively affected by PTSD. As a leader I did believe myself to be one who showed empathy and supported those who came to me with their concerns but I recognized my feelings of being un-easy by "dealing" with these Soldiers. I remember thinking "I rather deal with a mutilated Soldier, or one with a broken leg, than to deal with one who has not the ability to cope with his or her experiences" – Nevertheless, I was willing to listen and help but eager to do a "hand-off" to a higher authority or medical representative.

My return back home was uneventful. I rushed through the re-integration process that we were all made to go through, after all, I didn't need help. I was fine.

It was only about a month after my return that the "hey, can I talk to you" conversations started. It would start with casual conversations during work from Peers and subordinates. Mostly inquisitive in nature, the conversations would start with casual statements relating to events during the previous deployment. The conversation would inevitably would lead to statements that would lead me to as "are you ok?" – Statements such "things are so much different now", "I wish things were back to normal" or "life just doesn't seem right". I never understood why I feel compelled to ask the follow up questions since I knew it would require my involvement. I had to admit that I hated these encounters because I, myself, simply did not want to recall or pay attention to lingering thoughts of deployments past. I would listen, however, and send these Soldiers on their way to see a chaplain or a doctor. Although I listened, and I know they wanted to, I never talked about my experiences or feelings as it felt as though that action was... unfitting of me.

About six months had passed after returning when we were notified we would deploy again in less than 15 months. Shortly after that, the word spread. First about Suicide attempts which were often chucked off to "acting out" and about "weak" Soldiers just not wanting to participate in training. Soon after, evening formations would serve to notify entire sections that someone had passed away from a "suicide attempt" – few times, if ever, the death was acknowledged as an "deliberate suicide" but rather "an accident following an attempt or gesture".

Investigations always followed. More times that I'd like to remember I'd be sitting down in some office being asked questions as to my conversation with an Soldier on the days or months leading to his or her suicide. I always got asked the same questions "why did they talk to you?", "what did you talk about?", "did they share their plan?", "what happened in Iraq?", "do you think you did everything in your power to prevent this?" The truth was; I never really knew why people talked to me, those who actually voiced things like "I'm done", or "I can't do this anymore", never actually shared a plan or actual intent, and the vast majority actually seemed quite... at peace, and calmed when sharing. Only one that I can remember ended up in the hospital for psychiatric help. The rest were released on their own, to their families, or their command shortly after.

My nights began to feel longer. Thoughts and conversations in my head replaying over and over, especially after the 3rd Suicide. Although we very, very seldom saw combat – Combat described by Soldiers as the actual engagement with an enemy, one that you can see and react to – we did frequently experienced what I began to refer to as "Cold Combat". While on dismounted patrols or driving on a convoy, IEDs or Improvised Explosive Devices would routinely destroy our vehicles and injure or kill Soldiers – Everyone was trained, ready, and able to fight, retaliate, win... however, following the death and destruction there was simply no one to fight, there was no army, no group, no gang, no team, not even an individual to retaliate or fight against. There was just quiet, frustration, anger with no outlet. Months after returning from that first deployment and after people began taking their own lives I realized that I was angry. Angry of returning home from a mission, a convoy, or a patrol with depleted medical supplies, dead Soldiers, and a full load of ammunition. I didn't' understand, however, why a Soldier would choose to end his or her life because of these feelings, further adding to my growing frustrations. I still, however, managed to sink myself deep into pre-deployment preparation, unknowingly neglecting myself and my family.

Not quite two years later I find myself a newly commissioned officer and on an Airfield preparing to, once again, mobilize to Kuwait prior to going into Iraq. I had now more responsibility and previous "combat" experience and I was, once again, dedicated, fearless, and willing to do my job.

I supposed I expected change, but the country looked and felt exactly the same. A strange familiarity that gave me some comfort and felt "right" to be there. My job had changed to an "advice and assist" capacity, which for me meant assisting with the development and re-establishment of Iraqi, host nation, medical capabilities. We'd recruit Iraqi doctors, nurses, and other medical staff displaced by the original conflict and provide a safe place for them to work. This usually meant safeguarding re-constructed hospitals and clinics. We would no longer take injured civilians to U.S. or Coalition medical facilities and I was to encourage that the local populace relied on their own medical system. Suicide bombers and IEDs were routine in crowded markets, government buildings, and police stations.

We were tasked with responding, securing, and evacuating people from these sites to local Iraqi health care facilities. Men, women, and children of all ages fell victims to these senseless attacks and in vast numbers. Crowding injured and dying in our vehicles as well as civilian vehicles, my Soldiers would exhaust every ounce of energy, medical equipment available, and patience on the overwhelming multitude of injured and dying while local medical response teams would simply refuse to show up to the scene or leave their posts at hospitals under threat of retaliation by local insurgents. The anger of my Soldiers quickly turned to me after, one by one, people would begin to die from injuries sustained. My requests for air or ground assistance denied as part of an Iraqi "self-reliance" strategy.

As supplies dwindled and people succumbed to injuries, Soldiers began the difficult task of separating those who would die from those who had a better chance if treated quickly. Locals quickly learned what the markings meant - small letters written with sharpies on foreheads- The dreaded "E" for expectant, we would no longer spend efforts or supplies on anyone with this marking. Angry parents trying to save their children, wives pleading for their loved ones. I was the immovable force to say "No" – to off load dead or dying as we slowly sent people to whatever hospitals or clinics still had an ill-trained, staffed, or equipped medical team or provider.

This type of event, unfortunately, repeated itself throughout the deployment. Once again, no one to shoot at, to hold responsible for these actions. Quickly the resentment of my own Soldiers turned to me, for Soldiers are good, compassionate people, and the vast majority want to see those injured treated, even if they are not our own. I could not hold their feelings against them. I was frustrated by my inability to do more, and I had to hold my ground or orders given.

This "Cold Combat" would send people spinning out of control, causing fights and endless arguments among the Soldiers. I was personally attacked more than once by my own Soldier's, angry, and frustrated for "not doing the right thing" – particularly after an event where a young Iraqi man on his 20's approached the hastily constructed entry control point to what later would become a large forward operating base. The man had both hands missing. Escorted by his wife and two other men with superficial injuries they approached the gate with no shirts and their pants legs rolled up to show they were unarmed. With some proficiency in the language I was called to the gate to find out what was the issue. The man's wife explained that the husband had been working on a gas stove that exploded and took both of his hands. We had all seen this before, the man was likely setting up low-grade roadside explosives or door/window explosives targeting our patrols. Something went wrong, the device detonated and took his hands. Protocol directed full treatment and evacuation for these "suspects" for further processing and interrogation. To Soldiers around me however, this meant that we finally had a "culprit" someone to direct anger towards – "let him die", "why are we going to treat him" – I ordered treatment and full evacuation, earning me a very difficult position to be in. That night, a Young Soldier, about 19, pointed his rifle at me. Tearful and full of anger, he sat there staring at me for what seemed a lifetime. We didn't speak but I knew what he was thinking. That I was on "their side" – protected and saved this [Iraqi] man that likely had killed one of us in the previous weeks. He simply walked away. Sometime later, during that deployment, he shot himself.

It was during this deployment when I began to doubt my position, my purpose, and my feelings on this... war.

I began to feel guilt, although I'm not exactly sure what about. I had become an outsider, an American

Soldier in Iraq, mistrusted by the locals as well as an outsider among my own Soldiers.

Like a bad dream, the re-integration process was painfully familiar. Medical and psychiatric questions. In a rush to get done and being released to go home we (I) rushed through exams, questionnaires, and surveys. A sign on the Gym's wall read "Asking for help is a sign of strength" – It never occurred to me to "talk to someone" but the truth is that I was bothered by many events, circumstances, and interactions for that past year. I waited on one of five chairs outside of an office labeled "Community Mental Health", taped to the door on a printed piece of paper. There were two other Soldiers there. I asked how long they had been waiting and the younger of the two simply stated "forever". About ten minutes had passed when an irritated-looking gentlemen opened the door, looked at his watch, glanced at the three of us and turned to the young Soldier directing others to wait for mental health if they wanted services- A Soldier left his officer stating "don't bother" – The gentlemen, I assumed was either a psychologist or psychiatrist, told the NCO that "it is now 1630hrs, why are you still directing people to come see me? The two Soldiers waiting for him angrily got up and walked away- I was about to do the same when he asked me "what do you need, I have ten minutes if you hurry up!" – I walked away to go find the two Soldiers that had left. I caught up to one of them, a slender tired-looking older Sergeant. I asked if he was ok and apologized for the Doctor's behavior. He didn't say anything other than "it apparently doesn't matter, is 1630, sir!" – I didn't know that to say.

It took me a few days to realize that I was rather upset at the fact that I wanted to vent. I wanted to be listened to and felt as though what I was feeling did not matter. After all, if you had chest pain you were immediately sent for an exam, if you had muscle or joint pain, difficulty breathing, or any other physical illness there was not a shortage of personnel at the ready, regardless of time of day. Why was wanting to talk any different? – This thought process was quickly, on the drive home, replaced with "what was I thinking??" I don't need to talk to anyone and embarrass myself, I just need a good dinner, go out, have fun! No?

The nights became very loud. More specifically, silence became very loud. The stillness of home, no generators humming, no constant back and forth of vehicles and the sound of steps at all hours of the day became very uncomfortable. Obsessive thoughts became the norm while trying to sleep. Conversations, decisions, and arguments. What I could have done, what I should have done. My bed became uncomfortable and began sleeping in the couch. Somehow a crowded space was comforting rather than the expanse of a king-sized bed. Sleep became a luxury and I began to sleep less and less. I hated thinking about things but missed being deployed. Hated not being home, but was uncomfortable now that I was.

After 30 days off, following deployment I looked forward to going back to work. 12 hour (or more) days were normal and I didn't mind. I was busy and my worries and obsessive thoughts began to fade away. At some point, months later, I can honestly say I almost didn't think about anything relating to past deployments at all.

Seven or so months had gone by. Soldiers came and went. New faces made things normal again, like nothing happened. I have always disliked social media and, to this date, I do not have a Facebook, Instagram, etc.. However, most people do. News reached me through casual conversations that a Soldier assigned to my platoon during the previous deployment had been found by the State Police, single shotgun shot to the head, self-inflicted. Local news called it "a disturbed Soldier's suicide" following his wife leaving him. Reports later stated that his wife had grown tired of deployments and we had, once again, just been notified of another deployment coming up. I recalled that months before he had mentioned that his wife had been upset at how often we deployed, his "lack of caring" after coming back from deployments, and that arguments were a common fixture in their relationship. Although I remember the conversation I cannot remember what, if anything I said to him. I began to think that maybe my lack of support or something I said could have contributed to this. Intrusive thoughts about deployments, began flooding my mind once again.

It started with the smell. In my own room, in my home, at work, or driving, something as simple as sand in the air, the metallic scent of blood, or the smell of diesel, would send me back to remembering events although I could no longer remember which deployment the memory belonged too. Obviously the scent was in my own mind, which made the memory that much more disturbing. I thought to ask for help but what was I going to say? "I smell things that aren't there?" –

The next deployment could not come fast enough. Between preparations, training, and coordination I had no time for thinking, resting, remembering.

This time, however, is the first time that I was apprehensive about going back. The "Iraq Surge" they called it. Another 12 month deployment which would turn to 15 at month 9. This time, with a completely different objective for my unit. We were to take over homes and territory in the south-western provinces of Iraq in order to build a presence and attempt to curve the growing insurgency. Nothing changed. Our Soldiers would die and there would be no one to shoot at, for the most part. Nevertheless I immersed myself in work, in helping others to "be better" and "make it through". I made other Soldier's problems my own and spent my energy and resources to "help" – I know now that this was my way to avoid my own needs and to adamantly refused to ask for help. Everyone needed help. Not me.

As much as I try to remember this, very long, deployment I cannot. I have short memories of days, events, faces, and conversations but I cannot or will not remember as I think I should. We all saw death, received injuries, fought, and went through it but I feel as though I was there in mind only, observing. Like it was a dream.

Like the deployment itself I don't remember the home-coming. I do recall that this time I'd be leaving my home station and heading to Germany. I was excited. No more deployments, no more being away from home. I never realized how much this transition would affect me.

An assignment to a non-combat unit was supposed to be a "break" but it turned out to be anything but. My first month of work came with the realization that I'd never go back to being deployed. No more pre-deployment training, no more "deployment cycle". The relief was short-lived. The constant flood of memories, all unrelated and seemingly incoherent constantly distracted me from work, from home, from life in general. I became irritable, anxious, and generally unhappy. Busy, once again, solving everyone's problems but my own and neglecting my own family I started to descent into a state where I could not stand to be with myself in a room. A doctor's visit for constant headaches, lack of sleep, energy, and weight gain ended with a referral to mental health.

"You might have PTSD", I was told. To which I replied, "that is for people that are scared of something that happened and don't want to go back" – I wanted, and still do, want to go back! So I can't have PTSD, right?- Insulted, I didn't go and continued to refuse for two years.

I tried to fix myself. In denial and in secret, like as If I was doing something illegal – I read the books, I went to leadership seminars and talked to others. I was steadily doing worse and no longer being able to concentrate on work, family, life. Then it happened; suicide wasn't dumb, not selfish, nor cowardly! It is a personal decision and who is who to judge anyone?! – Is easier than being exhausted and not sleep, been hungry even though you eat and eat, easier than trying to explain what you think to anyone, surely easier than thinking, thinking all the time about everything and nothing. Simpler than pretending that helping other people with their problems is for them rather than a way to make me feel better about... something. The thought caught me by surprise. I was both terrified and ashamed.

I have support. I have people that love me. A loving wife who has not given up on me when she has nothing but reasons to quit. I have wonderful children and some would tell me I have a bright future. I just can't see any of it. How can you say things like this to people that are trying to support you? – I finally agreed to "get help". It has been a difficult road and I still can't say things will be ok. I despise being labeled but I could not continue to live with sudden and uncontrollable periods of crying for no reason, of being angry at nothing. I was finally one of "those guys" – weak and broken. Haunted by memories that do not really make much sense and deafened by silence. Maybe I should have been stronger and admit I had difficulties much sooner, maybe I should not have re-enlisted, or commissioned. All I can do now is allow myself to be helped which is, in itself, very traumatic.

So now, at the end of my career, I have surely skidded in broadside, used up physically and mentally worn out. The ride isn't over but it has been a ride that I am not sure I'd have taken if I had known.

:::
:::::::::::::

So, I ran into my friend with the diary again and here is a guy that's always smiling and cheerful and thinks life is good and says he feels so blessed. So I'm thinking ok so why search me out cause it seems that I run into him a lot and that every now and then when meet and something inside changes. Anyway this time he started telling me about this woman that had been shot twice by Sadam's elite guard or something and she was pregnant and all the stuff they did to keep her and her fetus alive. I thought that was pretty rough thing for all concerned to go through. He had that damn diary and share that with me;

Good Morning little girl, good Morning Tony boy, well guys I really ended up earning my keep yesterday, Today is March 16, 10:15 AM as soon as we got to Romeo I knew it was going to be a long day (we flew 9.5 hrs) we completed 3 missions before we had to Stop for aircraft maintenance it was 1:30 AM and we were closed To our home base (charlie) so we decided to sleep a little and return To Romeo in the Morning after the AcFT was ready but this morning we got a different acFT so Now we are on our way back To Romeo, when we landed yesterday I went in to see if There were any patients for us To Transport out when I got there They had a Woman on the operating table she was 4 Months pregnant and had been shot in the leg and on the left side right below the Rib cage when I

got there they already had her all
opened up They took her intestines
and stuff and lay them on the
outside of her so they could have
room to go in and look for the
bullet plus suture everything that
had been torn up by the bullet, it
was really something to see cause
you could see the fetus in the
sac they (The Doctors) did a good
job of sewing up the wounds and
cleaning it up, when they were done
they put the intestines and stuff
back in and sewed her up again
the fetus seemed to be doing fine
I took some pictures of the whole
procedure that might seem gross to
some people but I think its something miraculously beautiful the way God
Lets us be able to work on the different parts of the body in so many
different ways in order to preserve
Life as he wills it. any way we
waited about an hour after surgery
before trying to Evac her to a

better place cause she really needed
to be on a fetal monitor and other
stuff that we don't have in the field
out here, I really had my hands full
we ended up transporting her before
she was really stable because we had
another Iraqui brought in with a
sucking chest wound with a trache-
otomy done and massive head injury
plus a lady with an 11 month old
boy who had swallow sort kind of
caulking compound and was going through
convulsions plus one other Iraquie
with an old gunshot wound through
his elbow, we didn't expect the
guy with the head injury to live
through the ride and didn't know
if the pregnant lady would make
it or if the 11 month old would make
it either, I had like 8 I.V's going
at once hanging all over the helicopter I told the lady (through an
interpreter) to try to grab the babies
Tongue and keep him from swallowing
it if he went into convulsions

and halfway through the flight I
ran out of oxygen that I was giving
the pregnant lady but she still
made it as well as all the others,
when I dropped them off I went
in to give the doctors information on
them and they took off a bandage
that was covering the head injury
of the one guy (actually he was just
a kid about 14 or 15 yrs old) anyway
I didn't think he would make it
much longer and if he lived he
would be a vegetable because
the left side of his skull was frac-
tured and most of his brain was
hanging out all shredded, before
I left I gave the lady with
the 11 month old one of my wool
blankets cause it was pretty cold
and she didnt have anything to keep
them warm, boy was she ever grateful
for that and everything else they
are all so grateful, I'm glad that
they get a chance to see that
we are not the infidels that

they are told we are, I hope they get peace in their country soon. we hauled a few more urgent patients like I said we didnt get done till 1:30 AM, oh the guy with the gunshot to the Elbow kept trying to tell me something throughout the flight, Toward the end he started screaming and getting angry and I didnt have any morphine or valium to shoot him up with I thought he was having pain from his injury but when I was in the Evac hospital I found out that it was that he had to go ~~the~~ to the latrine, well we just landed at ponvo let me go in and see what if any injured they have for me

I love you and miss you

Daddy

I served in Desert Storm as a medevac pilot. Most of the wounded I carried were Iraqi soldiers, enemy combatants. I saw horrendous injuries in those days, more than I ever expected when I first got into my helicopter. I witnessed surgeries on civilians, prisoners of war, and our own soldiers in the hospital tents. During the surgeries the tents would fill up with dust and sand due to the high winds. I asked one of the surgeons that had to stand on a crate because he was so short, how can they survive in such an unsterile environment, and he just stated they fill them up with antibiotics. I know it sounds crazy but when I was between missions, I would go into the surgery tents and observe. It was fascinating but very sad!

Some memories have faded but some remain sharp as

if it happened yesterday! One is of a pregnant woman, six or seven months along, who had taken shrapnel when Saddam Hussein's forces fired on villages protesting his rule. She survived, by some miracle, but the image of her abdomen cut open and you could see the uterus while the surgeon was feeling around for shrapnel and by some miracle it was not punctured! To this day I wonder if she and her baby survived.

The children stay with me too. Many had shrapnel wounds from the same attacks. Sometimes we carried two children on a single stretcher. That is a sight you will never forget.

remember one boy in particular that was full of shrapnel from an attack by his own people, the Republican Guard. His parents had been killed; we carried his aunt and uncle in the same helicopter. When I went to check on him in the hospital tent, I was still in my flight suit, survival vest, sidearm, and gas mask. My motor pool sergeant had handed me a small stuffed animal to give to the boy after I told him the story. When I reached inside my flight suit to pull it out, his aunt and uncle got very scared, unsure of what I was reaching for. When they saw the toy, they relaxed, and the boy's eyes lit up, It was as if he had never seen a toy in his life. He smiled, even though he was wrapped in bandages. I will never forget that expression. I always wondered if he became a terrorist.

Not all memories are ones I want to hold onto. Some wounds required amputations, and the remains were bagged for disposal. Wild dogs would tear into the bags so at some point the decision was made to burn them. It is not a sight, or a smell, I care to remember but I remember it like it was yesterday.

We were lucky to have a commander who truly had our backs. When higher-ups wanted us to take experimental anti-nerve-agent pills and not record it, he refused. He made sure everything was properly documented, even the anthrax vaccines. I never took the pills myself; the side effects affected night vision, and we were already flying in dangerous conditions.

Leadership matters in preventing PTSD but sometimes nothing can prevent it. You never know how someone will respond to blood, to the sight of a wounded soldier being pulled out of your aircraft, to the open wounds caused by shrapnel, bombing and just plain combat. And sometimes trauma comes not from the enemy, but from your own side. Two soldiers once decided to play quick-draw. One didn't realize he had a round in the chamber. He shot his friend in the head. How does anyone survive witnessing that or killing your friend?

Flying was its own risk. We flew at night under NVGs, with no GPS, through sandstorms and rainstorms, sometimes lost in complete darkness. Flash floods would carve out the desert floor or cover roads that we used as checkpoints, and on a couple of occasions we'd land with barely enough fuel after failing to locate the Forward Area Refueling Point (FARP). I recall landing 18 minutes into my 20-minute light! I asked my crew if they wanted to continue to fly until we ran out of fuel and had to autorotated to the desert or to keep looking for the FARP. The risk was landing in a possible minefield, so we continued and found the FARP.

Yet amid the chaos, we found ways to relieve some of the stress. The cook saved leftover fruit and fruit juices, I bought yeast in one of the local villages, and we made homemade hooch, something like a warm, gritty wine cooler. It didn't taste that good, but it was something. It brought us together.

Being reservists helped. Many of us had careers waiting at home. A sense of purpose to return to. Others weren't so fortunate, those who lost businesses, jobs, or relationships seemed to struggle the most.

Do I have PTSD? I think about what I witnessed. I

wake up sometimes remembering the children, the pregnant woman, the surgeries, the faces. I was lucky, I never had to kill anyone up close, but I saw what war does. The bombing, the artillery, the explosions... and the aftermath.

There were good days too, desert parties that felt like scenes from *M*A*S*H, playing cards in the tent until an alarm went off warning of a possible gas attack. Then we'd mask up and sometimes sleep in our chemical suits, sweating through 100-degree nights.

Those memories, good and bad, are all part of my story our story. They shaped me, haunted me, strengthened me, and stayed with me long after we returned home. Again, I'm a lucky one, I never had to beat in a door not knowing what or who was on the other side waiting to kill me. I was able to survive nearly a 30-year career as a soldier, pilot without ever having to kill someone, I was able to save lives and that is my happy ending.

CW4 Thomas Gasparolo

Moment of repose ....?

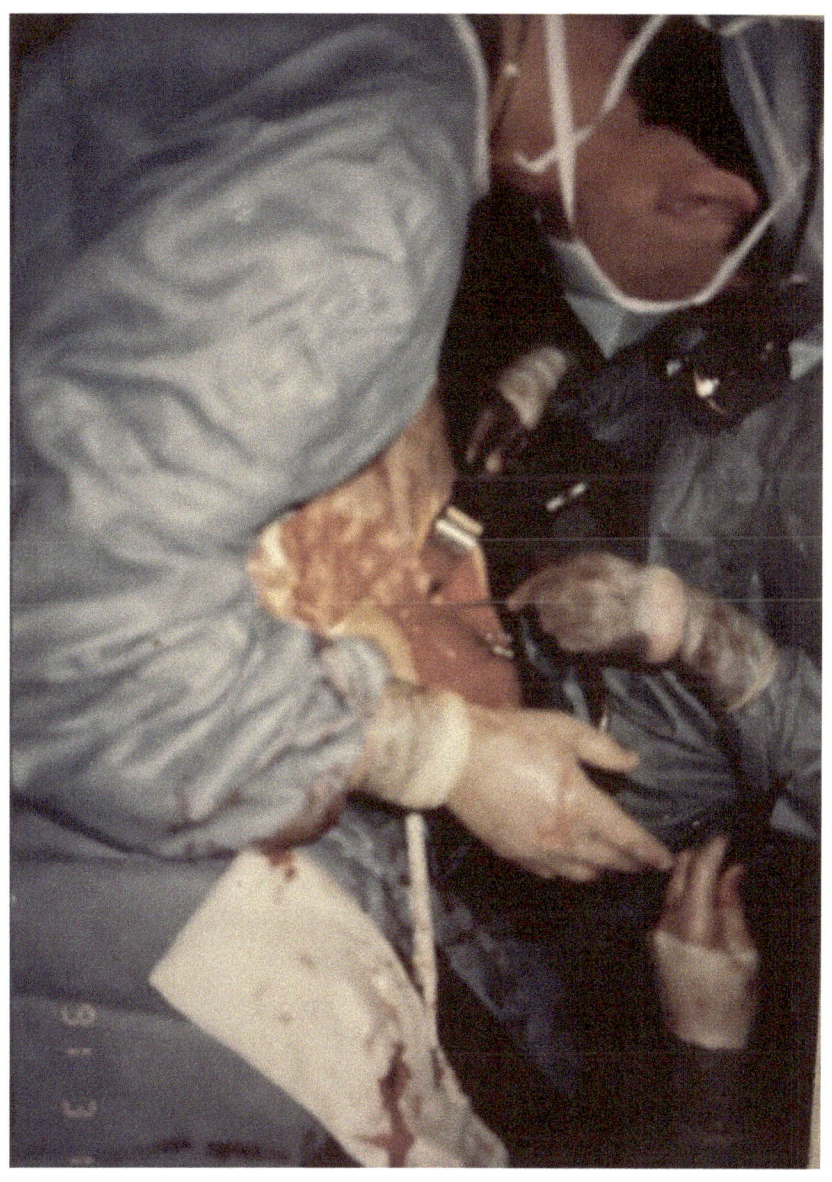

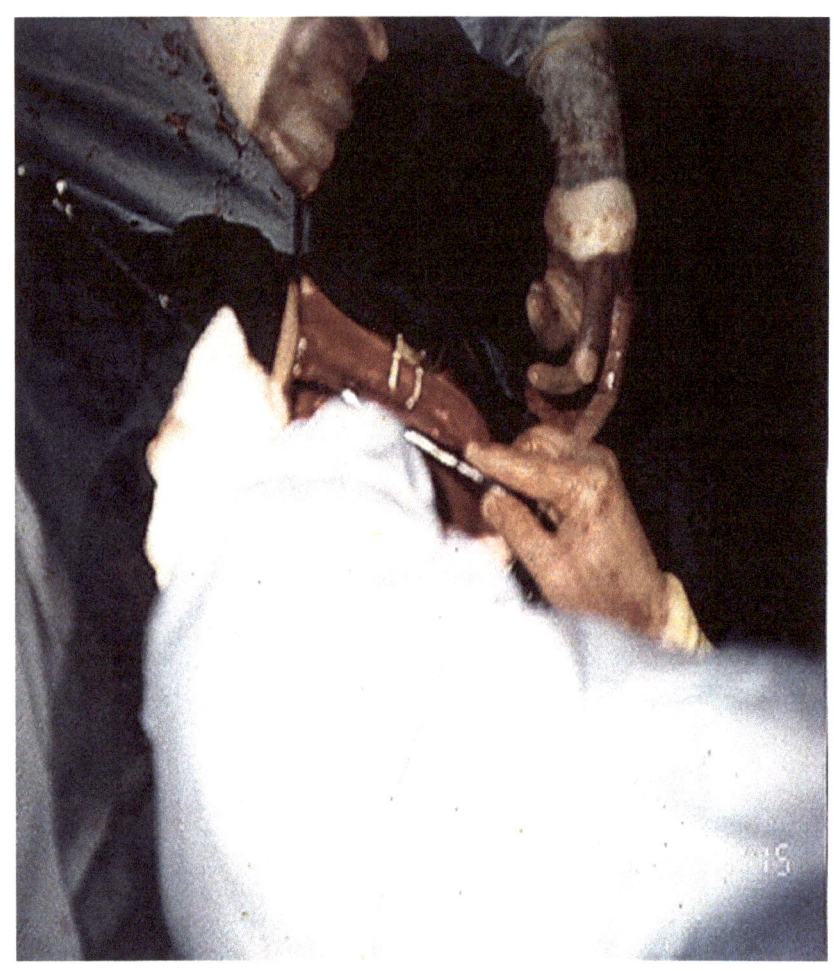

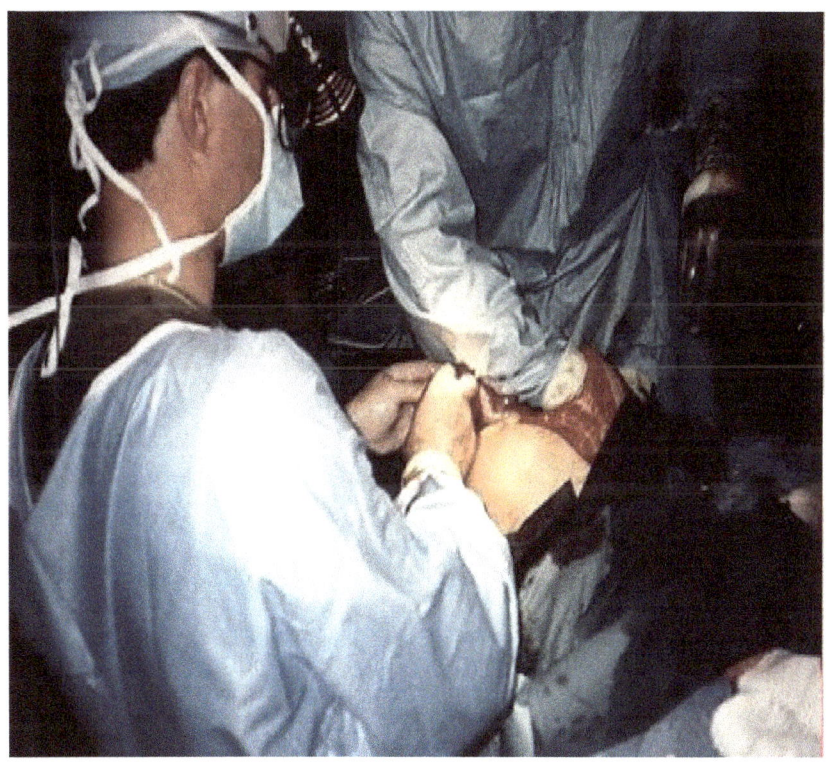

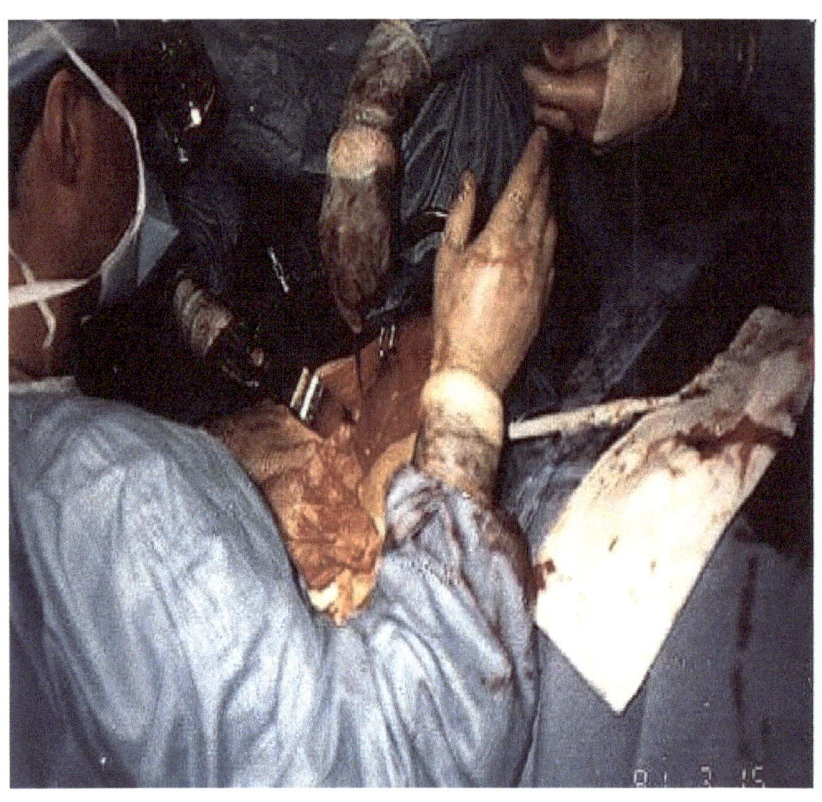

I Think My Friend has PTSD By Melvin Cintron

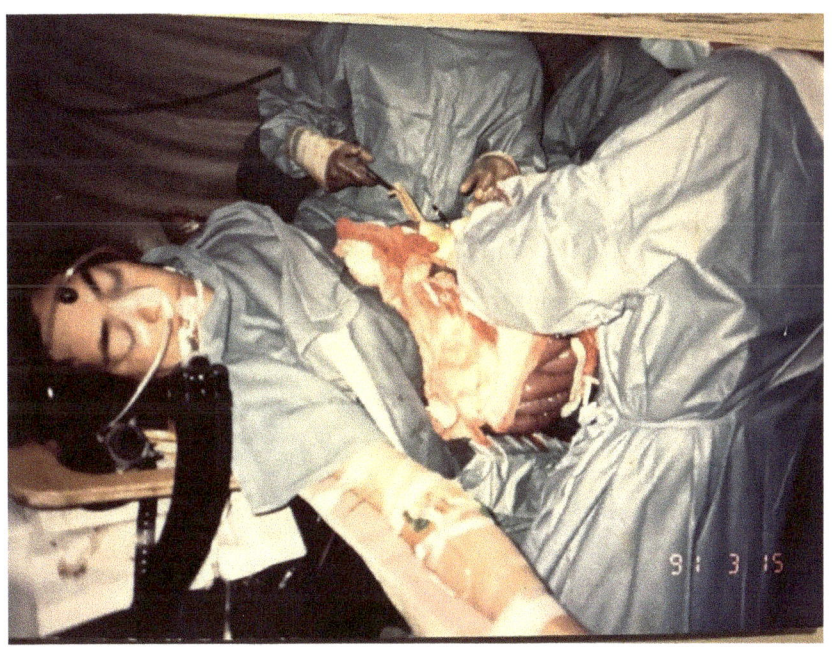

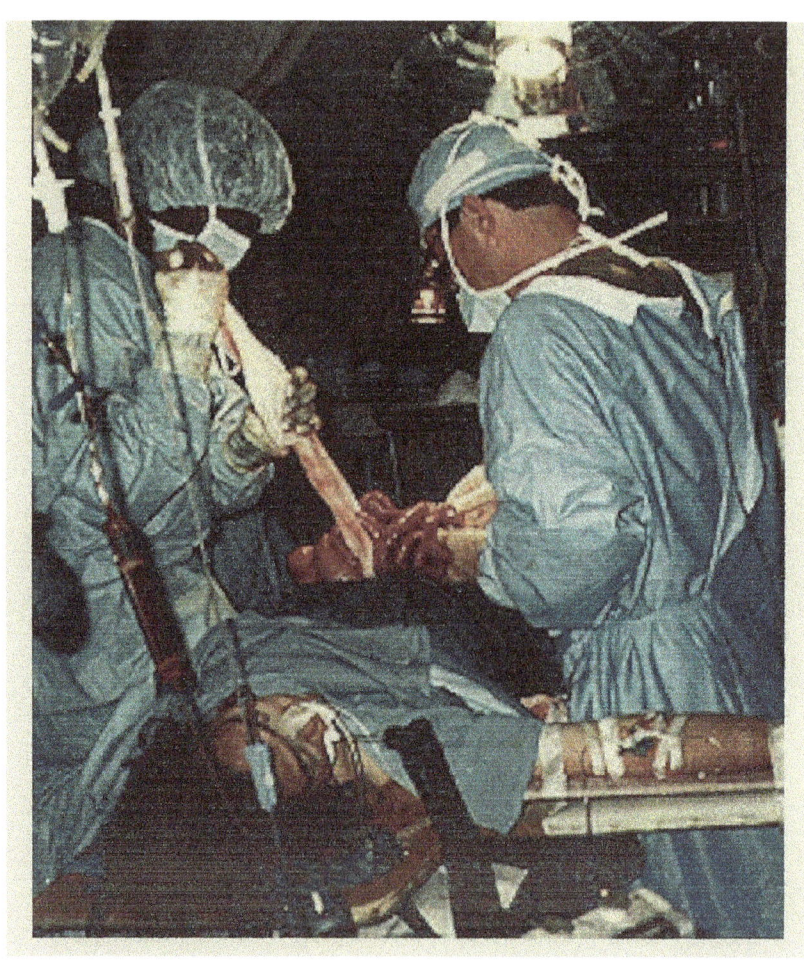

I Think My Friend has PTSD By Melvin Cintron

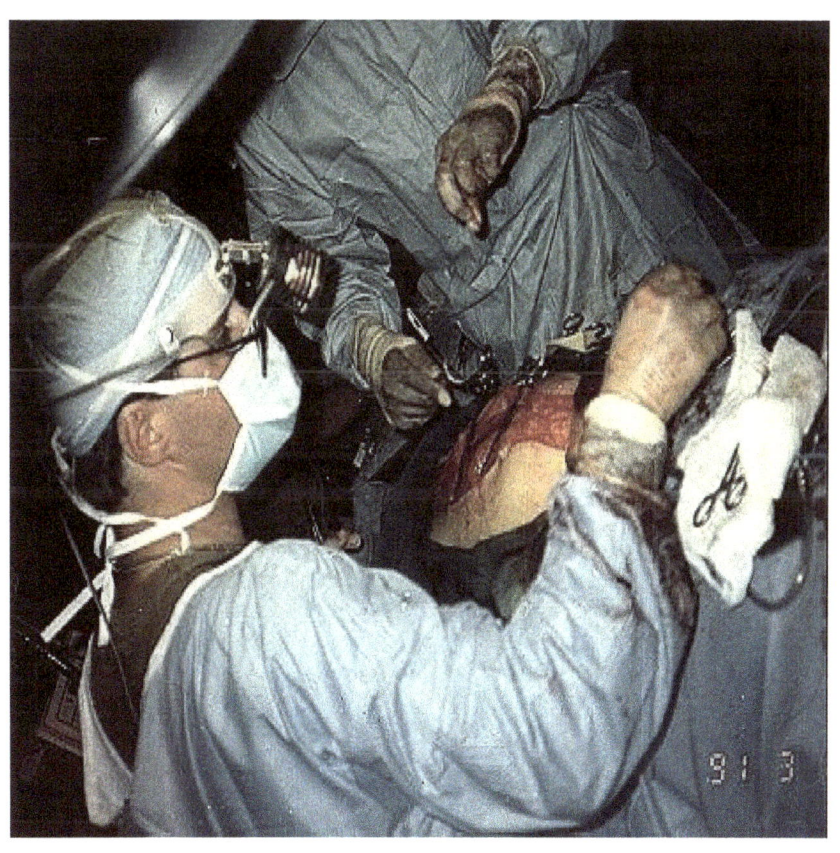

I Think My Friend has PTSD By Melvin Cintron

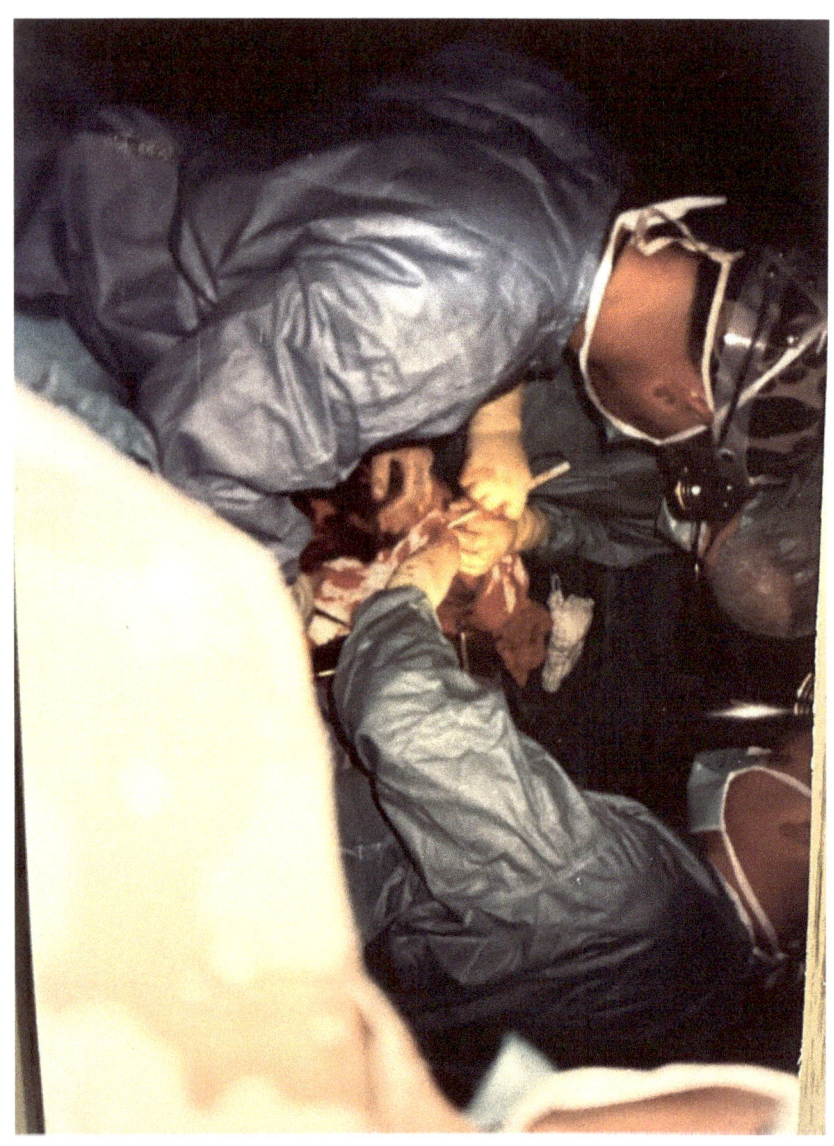

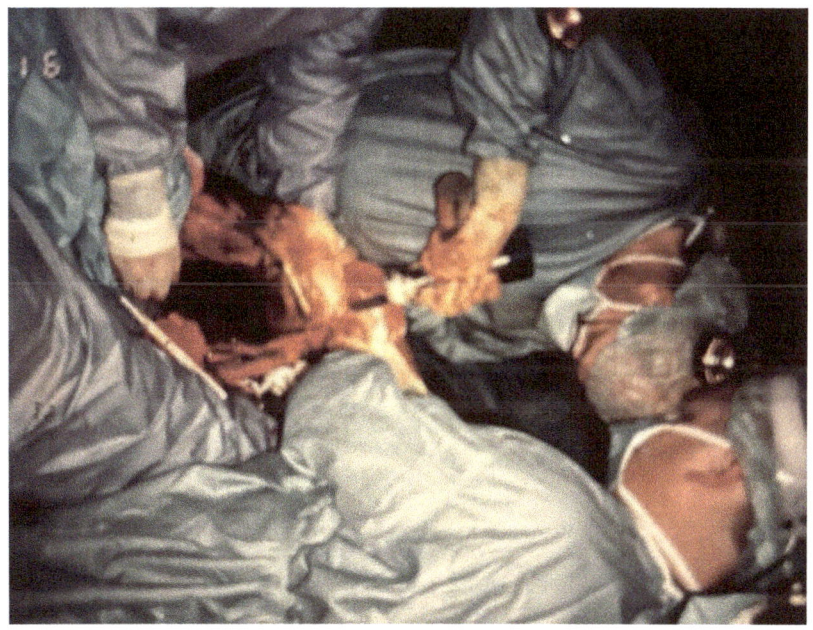

I Think My Friend has PTSD By Melvin Cintron

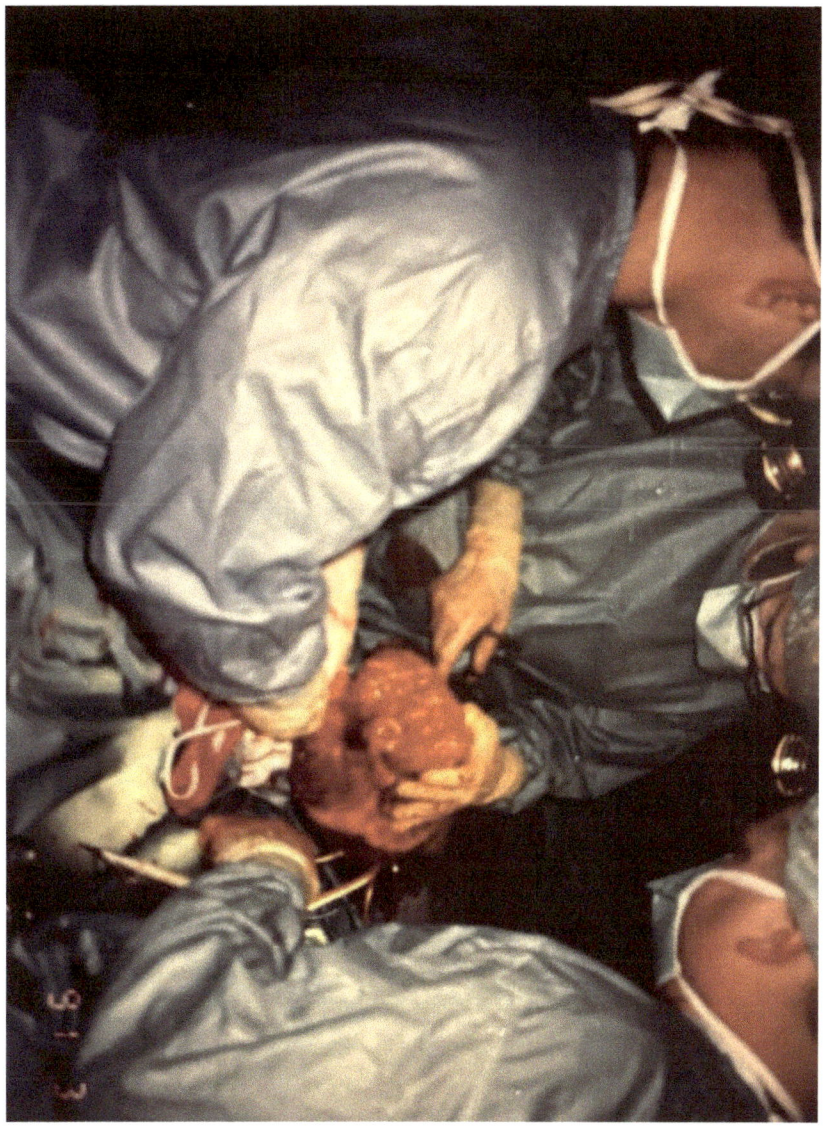

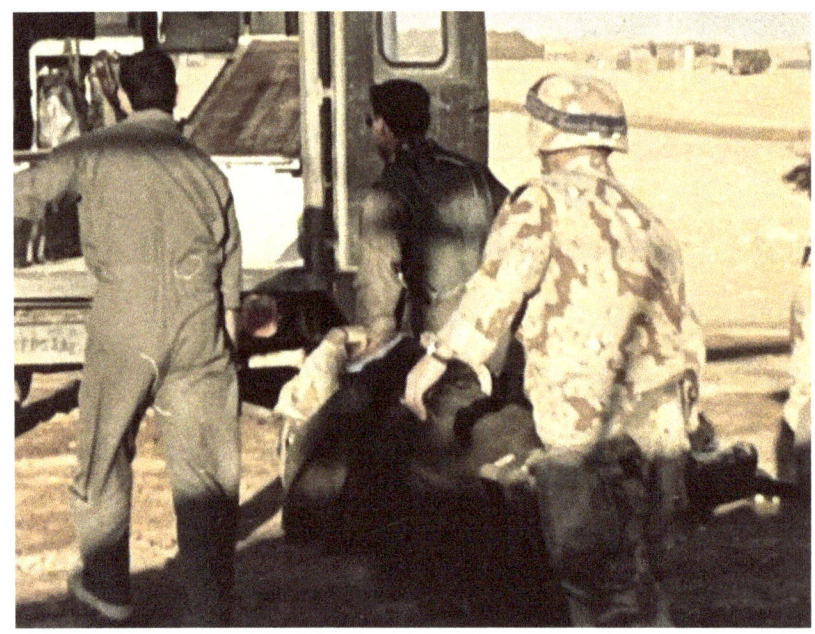

I Think My Friend has PTSD By Melvin Cintron

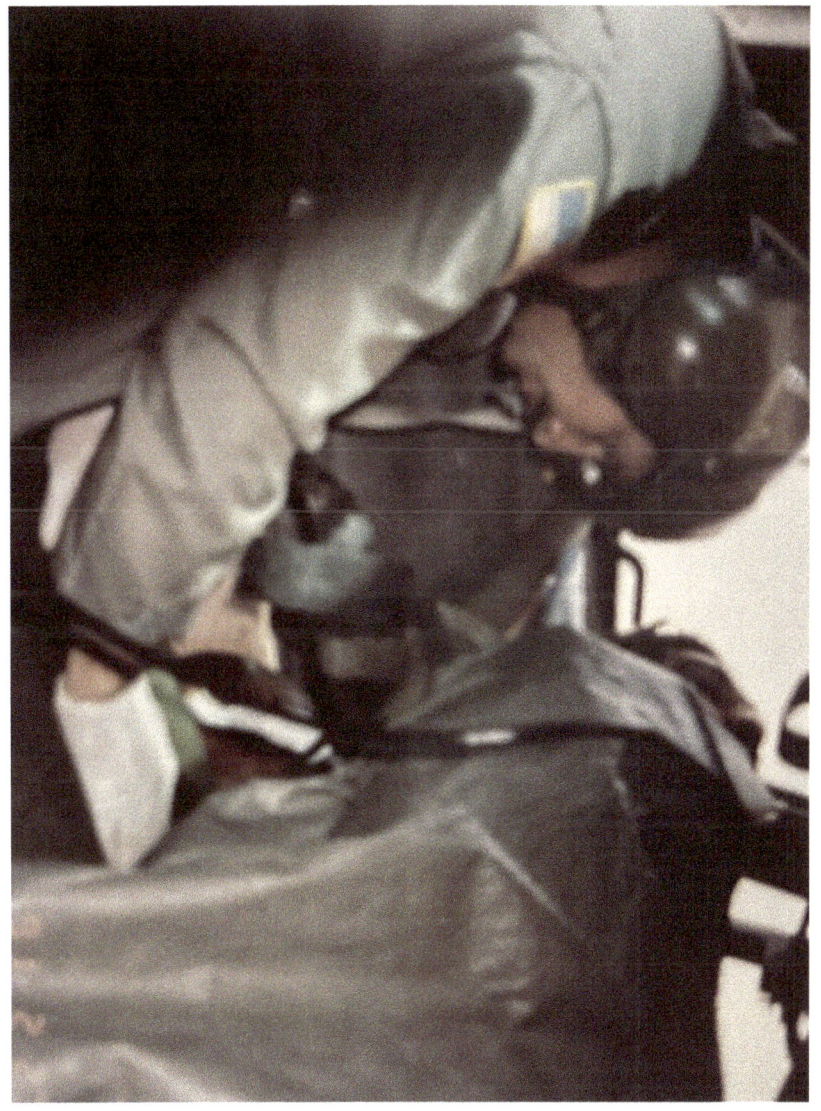

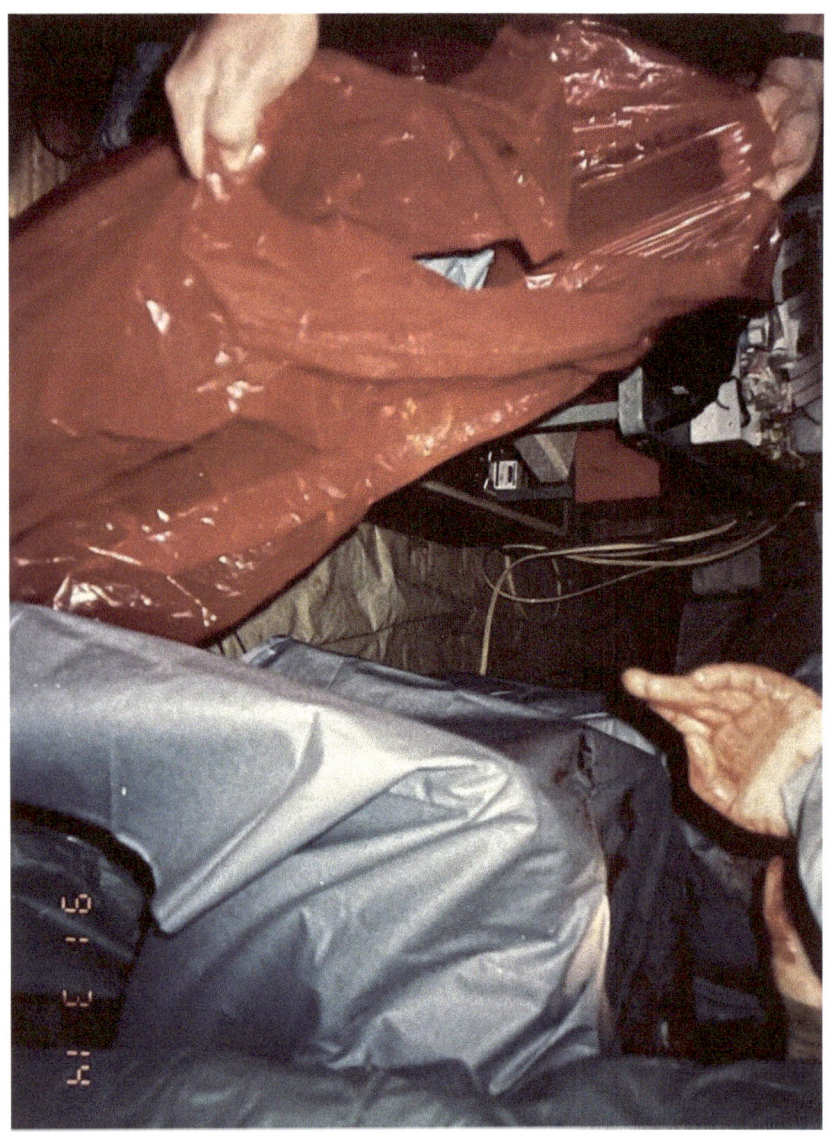

I Think My Friend has PTSD By Melvin Cintron

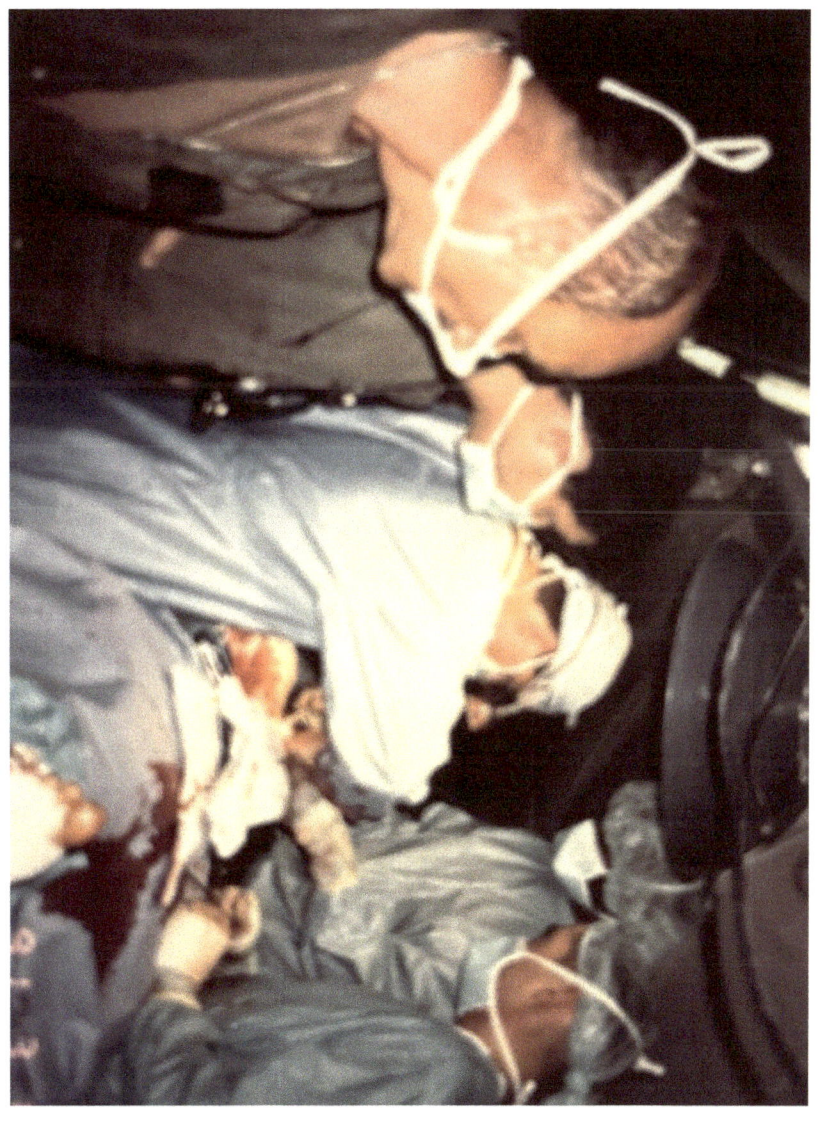

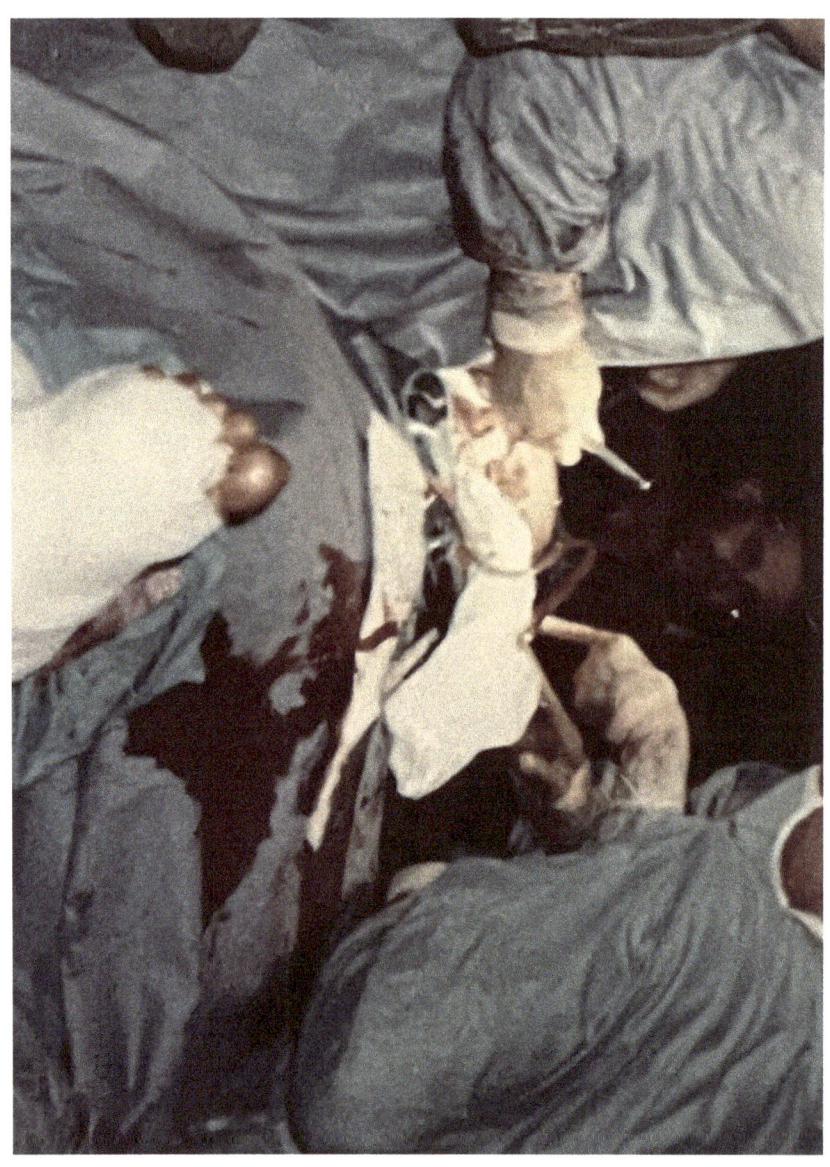

I Think My Friend has PTSD By Melvin Cintron

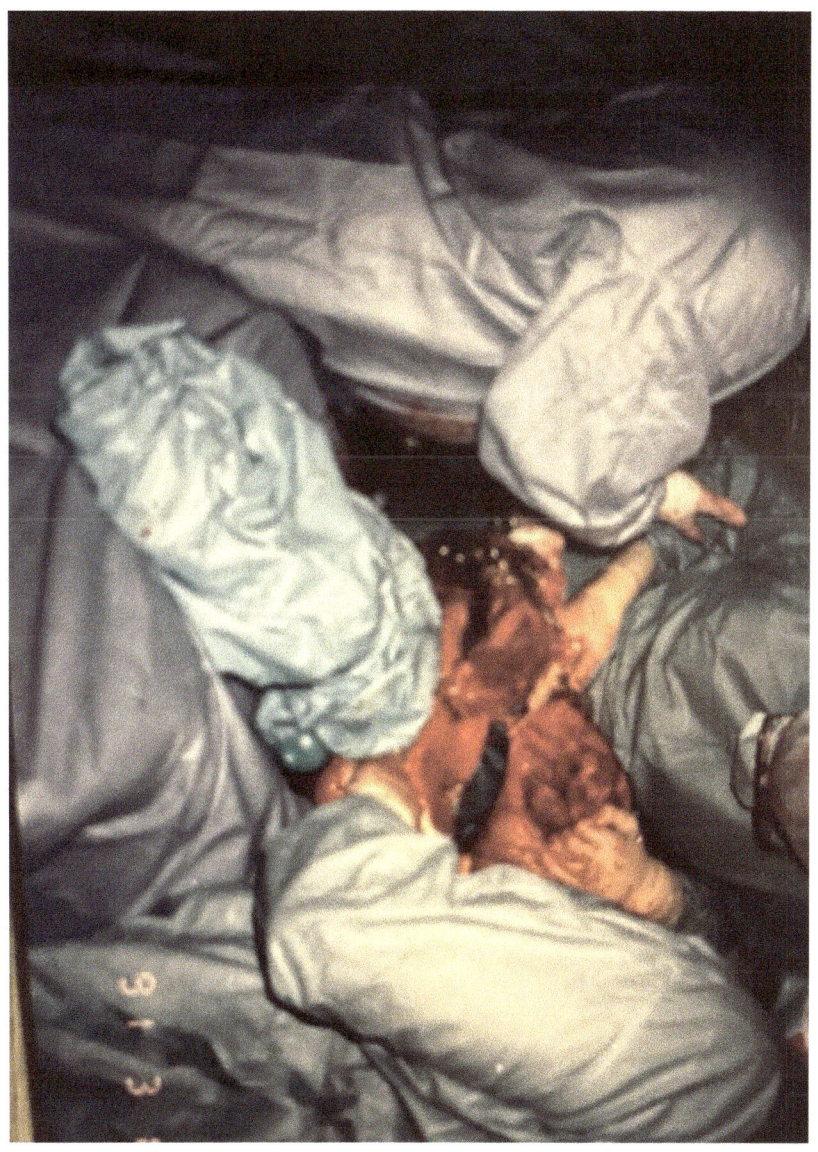

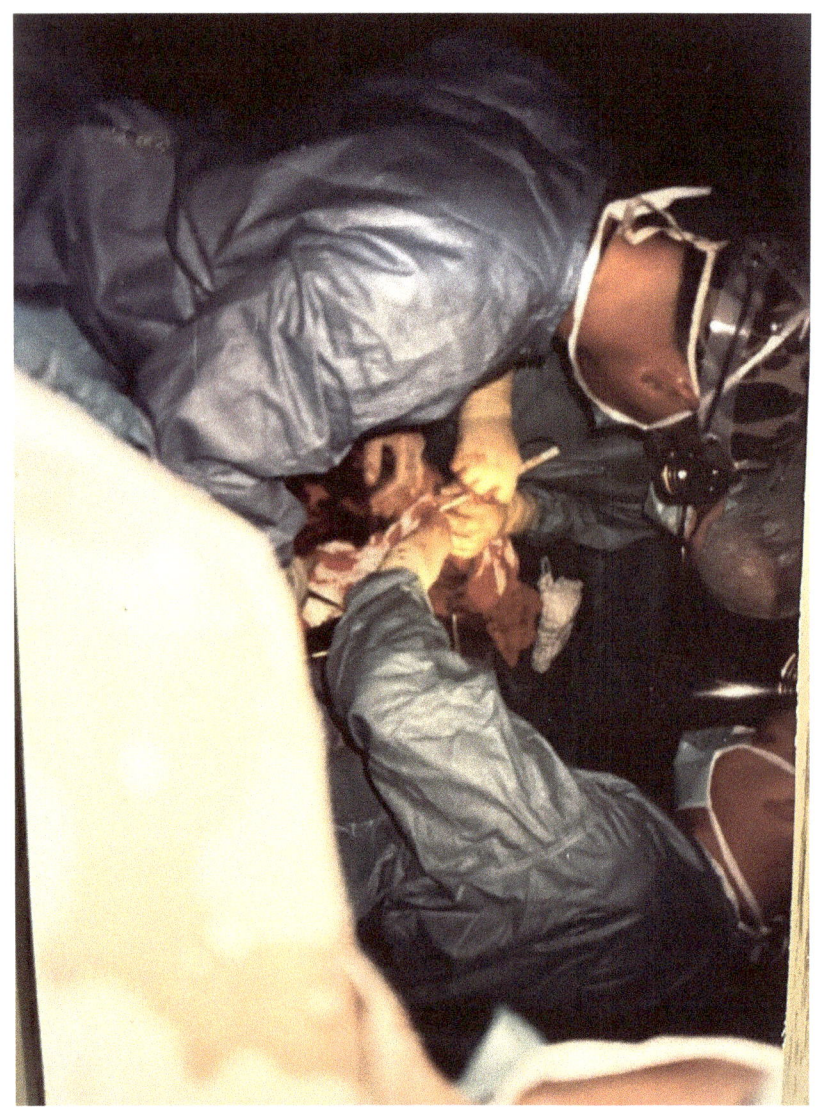

Ok I thought maybe this guy has seen more than my friend but I think my friend has more issues because I think my friend has PTSD. I need to help him and find a way to do it without losing my friend or our friendship. Anyway I figured I ask this guy about whether he is afraid of getting or having PTSD. Wow I kind of feel ashamed, I mean am I really talking about this the same way people talk about STDs? Gonorrhea, Aids I mean is it a disease or a condition to be ashamed off? I asked this friend if he thought he had PTSD and he said he always knew that he didn't come back the same person he left Hell if we got past AIDS being taboo shouldn't this at least sociably accepted without the having such a negative stigma around it?. Any way I did get interested in trying to figure out what he was doing and how he was dealing with his stuff to see if I could get some insights to help my friend.

I asked him if he thought he had a problem and man was I surprised at his answer. He said he knew even before the day he got on the plane back home, but he refused to admit or tell himself about it (which I found strange, I mean how the heck do you keep something you know about yourself from yourself?). Anyway he said the first time when he got home he used to talk to people about it, at times it was actually just kind of matter of fact but as time went by he noted that the more he talked about it the harder it was to talk about (isn't that contrary to what they say? He said the other two things he noted is that the more he talked about it the less he wanted to talk about it. The more he talked about it to get understanding the more he realized no one really understood. So I'm thinking this guy is no help as a matter of fact he is actually confusing me more than helping me. I said so did you stop talking about it (I mean he's not shutting up about it to me!). He said yes, and no, I stopped talking about it to others but it seemed I couldn't stop talking about it with me, to me (What!? What the hell's that mean? I thought). He kept going on and said sometimes I even felt embarrassed about telling someone and sometimes I felt like why did I even bother to tell that person or this person and kept thinking just don't say anything about it, it often made me feel like a weaker person, especially if someone really got me during one of those times when talking made me emotional. If I showed a certain level of emotion it would just bother me more that I gave in to talking that honestly about it. You know, sometimes I can talk about it almost un-emotionally, but sometimes, sometimes, well sometimes not, he said. I asked about his friends and he indicated that yeah there are some of them that you can talk to if they were there with you but even with them it's kind of a code talk we know we're drowning inside and we even say it's just that we say it but without saying it, we know it without really acknowledging how deep we know it, of each other, of ourselves, you know what I mean. You know what I mean he asks, you know what I mean? Hell No! I got no damn idea what your mean you're talking in damn circles. Why don't you guys just come out and talk and even break down with each other if you have to. I mean how can you be in that kind of stuff together or in the same type of shit and not be able to just be totally open about what it has done or it's doing to you. He said we do, we do just that, we just don't do it like that. By now I'm thinking, ok he is not really being much help on getting me to where I wanna be regarding helping my friend. But since I think my friend has PTSD and I wanna help her I kept listening, I mean maybe I'll end up with something helpful or something that I can use. After a while I tried to write about some of the things I felt or where inside me he said.

He said I even wrote poems about it and of course he felt compelled to share two of them following;

Callings

There are children calling my name
from beyond the warmth of the womb,

far below the light of unrehearsed

lullabies.

They cuddle around my nightmares and I cradle

them in the gashes of

my wounds.

There are children calling my name from the

corridors of my dreams,

seeking replies to answers that I forgot to question.

They crawl through the cracks in the walls of my

sleep and the

carcasses of their laughter fill the crevices of my

silence.

There are children calling my name

from within the innocence of their souls, past the

virginity of their

tears.

Yes, there are children calling my name and I grow deaf

but still there are children calling my name

and the more I grow deaf...the more I hear.

Crowded

There are children crying inside of me.

They take turns dying.

They visit my sleep, but their whispers

are all I hear.

Someday I'll name them.

Yes, someday I'll give them names to

die with.

My soul is crowded.

I look inside my soul and see so many tears from

children I didn't

know.

I try to hide within my sleep and dead memories

visit me. My soul is crowded.

Now I pray for empty spaces, for hollow thoughts,

for forgiveness of sins I did not commit, sins I

could not prevent.

Yes, I now pray for empty spaces within me and

still...

My soul is crowded.

Well that certainly seems to say something, I guess

(but then again what that something is, I have

no idea). I asked if he ever talked to a

professional and get help. He said he was

afraid of being labeled, he was afraid of

actually being told he had a problem, he was afraid of having something like that officially somewhere, being diagnosed and have to put that down in job questionnaires and stuff like that, having it follow him through his job or every time he tried to get a new job or promotion or something. Anyway he had ten thousand reasons for not doing it, so I a sked about his family. I said well if you wrote a diary for your kids and you have an issue that haunts you with kids how does that work out, are they older now can you explain it to them now, I asked him. He didn't really seem to want to answer that instead he asked me, how do you show such things that are inside you to your children, why would you even want them to see that, why would you want them to know, what good would sharing something like that do, how will they see you after that, and so on and so on. He had a barrage of questions like that which was not an answer or at least not the answer I was looking for (of course it's not like I knew what answer I was looking for anyway). So I asked about his wife and he said yeah I can talk to her sometimes but most times I talk to her through arguments it seems I can't or we can't talk straight about it till somewhere in the argument she says you need to get help or something like that which I take as no I haven't changed I don't need help you just need to, to I don't know what. Bottom line

he said, we definitely argue more, she says a

have a shorter temper that things seem to set

me off easier and I know she, and others, think

I've changed. And, and maybe I have changed

but even so I'm still the same I'm still me, just

different. At this point I'm thinking dude! You

are confusing the hell ought of me not really

helping my issue. I asked him if only the

children bothered him he said no, it all comes

to you every now and then, it's just that with

soldiers you can of know we are supposed to be

in harm's way and things like death and

injuries are almost an accepted part of our

reality. But innocent civilians, innocent

women and children, innocent children that have nothing to do with this, well seeing them, seeing their suffering well that is a little different. Seeing you buddies in all manner of different bad situations and even in the ultimate of situations, is actually no less painful and although it's supposed to be our reality, the reality is that it is no easier to accept, to live with. I guess it's all just as painful to know or to see or have been part of no matter how proud you are to have served to have done what you needed to do for you, your fellow soldier for others, for whatever.

I asked him about seeing a professional again and he told him the stigma stuff shouldn't be an issue people comprehend better than he thinks and they are more supportive and understanding of things like this than ever before. I asked him, haven't you seen that? Hasn't anybody come up and just thanked you for your service or done something similar. He acknowledged that yeah they, and they still do, and he feels grateful to them but more than that he feels guilty he almost feels ashamed, never of what he did or how he served but that he really doesn't deserve those thanks or praises he was just doing what we were all supposed to do and so many did so much more gave so much more and lost so much more, he said. He told me he had actually gone to the Veterans

Administration or military hospitals system but he always hated going there, it actually disturbed him to go. He said it was just too many issues with going there, he ended up feeling really anxious about being there, asking himself what he was doing there, did he really need to be there. It seems he always felt guilty about seeing other vets that really needed the help more than him because he had two good legs, two good arms, two eyes, hell he has a good job and supportive family so compare to others there he has no real problem there wasn't anything physical that he really had other than some joint pains and things that Motrim 800 could take care off, and maybe not being able to sleep well, sometimes not remembering things as easily, and his wife saying how he didn't have patience or got angry easier and seemed jumpy at times and some other stuff like that, but in reality he did not have the problems that these poor men and women di, because the fact was that he came back whole (at least according to him). So why should he be taking a space or time form doctors that have limited time to see soldiers or even civilian and others with real physical problems and things like that. I couldn't help but think that my friend didn't really have any "physical" problems either but here I am concerned as hell because I think that my friend has PTSD. Talking to this guy was actually letting me see some things that I was actually noticing in my friend. Anyway he dint seem to think much of the VA bureaucracy and he had a lot to say about that. Anyway he said one time he sat down and talked with someone that they scheduled him to talk to, must have been about 26 years old and never being in the soup or even deployed or even a traumatic situation, but the person really seemed to care and want to help but somehow it just seemed ridiculous to be talking to this person. He said that he got up and politely but very disappointedly left, even though he wanted to stay but how would talking to this unknowing person help how could this person relate, how is some degree supposed to now give him insight to what we have been through? Anyway he was concerned that what if something serious happens in the future and I can't take care of myself or I have to end up homeless or lose my house or something like that because of medical bills and stuff land it was all related to my service but it's too late for me to do anything about showing that? Specially if it's due to things that are from having served, but there is no record no determination, what if he really did need help and ends up not getting it. I said he shouldn't give up on the VA but he said he live with whatever it was he was living with since his firs deployment so many years earlier. He really was concern about what effect it could have on career and stuff how would a potential employer see it if he was diagnosed with something like PTSD, what if he needed a security clearance, what if, what if, what if, what the hell if?. There are so many potential issues with being labeled officially even to the point of being seen by others and by yourself as weaker, perhaps broken, perhaps unwell. I kept thinking man this guy may not be in some serious denial but he may definitely be seriously miss- informed. I mean can having or being diagnosed with PTSD really effect or have the negative impacts he is concerned with. How do people really look at it do they see him as weaker? Now that I think about it what about me and my friend am I going to see her as less if it turns out she does have PTSD, do I see him as less because I think he has PTSD? Do I think her weaker, I mean I'd still deploy anywhere with him and feel comfortable that she's got my back and stuff.

I asked if this was about how others, at home, at work, etc would see him or was it about how he would see himself? Was it really about the career concern. I believed him when he said it really was about all those things and quite a few others. I also believed that there's no way its gonna effect job things there are so many employers that actually have re-integration and veteran enabling and supporting programs. But after a few more references to this it became clear that he was not convinced of that.

Dear Hardy the baby,

its 21 March 920 P.M. we are on
our way back to Rovco we just
dropped off another load of patients
4 Iraquis and one American, the
American was a 1st Lt she had a broken collar bone, one of the Iraquis had a hand grenade explode
in his hand another one had
to have his arm amputated and
one had internal injuries there are
more injured Iraquis back at Rovco
but I dont know if we will eva-
cuate them tonight we are tired or
at least I am we had another
load earlier it was a pregnant
lady (full term) but her baby was
dead inside her for about 4 days so
we brought her in for surgical remo-
val of the fetus, another guy had
a broken foot, one a broken arm
and 3 old ladies one with fragmen-
tation to the chest, she was entubated
and one with cancerous tumor on
her toongue and nodules they

were all #ebated and all mal-
nourished one of the old ladies
(the one with cancer) was the
Mother of one of the guys with
the broken arms she cried a lot
but would kiss our hands because
they are so greatful for our help
its hard not to cry when you see
stuff like that, its easy to see how
these missions' can get to you after
a while, they are mostly all so
closed to dying they smell like
death, you dont feel like touching
anything with your hands even
after you wash them you think
there is still something there and
the smell stays in your mind so
long, but I guess its just another
expirience in life and to some
extent death also I have another
3 more days of these missions and
then its out of IRAQ and into
DAHRAN, saudi Arabia, to get ready
to ship ourselfs home, yes home
to my wife and children whom I love
above all earthly things.

Before you finish reading the Book...

All these years I've held off on finishing this book, how fullish of me thinking I'll go through it and fix the grammar, the past - present tense mistakes, the punctuation, the tremendously long sentences the overuse of commas, and everything else that I'm sure a publisher will recommend. Recommendations that will put this in a grammatically correct form. But there is nothing correct about PTSD no way to really eliminate the marks it puts on our lives no way to make it nice and neatly fitting into our selves. So as I'm writing I'm finally realizing that I am a friend that has PTSD and I realize that this is me, this is my insides, this is me crying, this is me hurting, this is me hiding, this is me visiting the dark places inside my mind, that I cant stop visiting, that I mustn't stop visiting, and hoping that I never stay in those dark places to long, this is me making believe its ok, this is me turning away help, this is me screaming for help, this is me hoping that no one will ever tell me again that they understand. This is me accepting, this is me crying in front of a friend, in front of my family, in front of my child, in front of my partner, this is me accepting that if they can't help they can care, this is me being ashamed of not having done more, this is me been proud of having done something, this is me being swallowed by survivors guilt This is me asking for help, this is me trying to help, this is me swimming in forgiveness that I give myself, this is me, this is me... drowning.

God Bless him and all the other doctors log-base

Romeo wish I could meet him again he did so

much to save as many as possible

Next to last Crew out Log-base Romeo

Excerpts of testimony before Congress, Warrant officer Cintron:

HEARING

before the

SUBCOMMITTEE ON OVERSIGHT AND INVESTIGATIONS

of the

COMMITTEE ON VETERANS' AFFAIRS

U.S. HOUSE OF REPRESENTATIVES ONE HUNDRED ELEVENTH CONGRESS

SECOND SESSION

———————

JULY 14, 2010

———————

Serial No. 111-91

STATEMENT OF WARRANT OFFICER MELVIN CINTRON, USA (RET.)

Mr. Cintron. Thank you. Mr. Chairman, distinguished Members of the Committee on Veterans' Affairs. My name is Melvin Cintron. I was a flight medic conducting forward area medical evacuation in support of U.S. and enemy wounded personnel, civilian, military and enemy prisoners of war.

I am also a veteran of Iraq Freedom War on Terrorism. I am extremely proud of my service to our country. I have been submitted for Combat Air Medal in Desert Storm and the Army Bronze Star Medal, which I did receive for my services in this last tour as an aviation maintenance officer.

I have no regrets for answering the call and would proudly do so again, despite the fact that it came at a great cost to me and my family financially, physically, socially and mentally.

However, I am often ashamed to enter the VA for help, having seen so many of my fellow soldiers that have paid an even much higher price for their service. I am here today in hopes that my testimony will help improve the support for them.

I would like to make clear that I personally know that the VA has many caring and committed professionals. My testimony is reflective of the system, not of the dedicated and committed personnel of the Veterans Administration.

When I entered the VA medical center, I see a poster saying, it takes the courage of a warrior to ask for help. But the poster should read, it takes the courage of a warrior to ask for help from the VA.

There are numerous examples of failures our veterans encounter when seeking help from the VA. But this Committee is seeking specific input on the VA's suicide prevention efforts and hotline.

Make no mistake, I consider myself extremely blessed. I have the ability to provide for my loved ones, two arms to hug my children, full sight to see my family, two legs which led me here to testify, not for my own need, but as stated, in hopes that in some way I can contribute to providing better support for others who may not be as blessed.

Their need for timely help from the VA should never be compromised. I feel strongly that the VA suicide prevention efforts and hotline are not working since it is too much of a last alternative with little else in between before getting there.

Have you heard the recording when veterans call the VA? Either you don't have enough of a problem and you can wait, sometimes for weeks for an appointment, or you're suicidal.

Distinguished ladies and gentlemen, I believe that there is a large void that exists between the no problem type strategy and the suicidal stigma strategy. Not having that void filled with intermediate prevention tools and mitigation strategies will only continue to fuel the need for the forensic type strategy of concentrating only on the suicidal hotline. I could easily be wrong, but I believe that by the time a veteran is desperate enough to call the suicide hotline, it may already be too late.

In my 19 years since coming back from Desert Storm, and my

5 years coming back from Iraq, I have met many veterans who have broken down while talking to me about their experiences, experiences they held for a long time. I have asked them, why don't you go to the VA for help, knowing the answer. I have advised them to call the VA, but they don't, because they are not suicidal and do not want to risk that label for fear of the effect on their jobs, their family, or social circles.

I have interacted with the VA regularly for many years, and I am aware of the suicide prevention hotline. However, I do not know of a readily or easily accessible intermediate or nonsuicide hotline. I apologize for my ignorance if such a system does exist. But if it does, and so many don't know of it, then the system obviously needs better marketing, promotion, and outreach, or at least as much as is done with the suicide hotline.

Instead of just suicide hotline, we should provide support long before a veteran considers suicide. Veterans need and deserve a system of continuing support, a dignified program that addresses basic needs of a soldier to talk without the stigma or label of being considered a suicidal risk.

Please help our veterans ask for help in dignity, not in fear, apprehension or labeling. Thank you very much.

[The prepared statement of Warrant Officer Cintron appears on p. 51.]

Mr. Mitchell. Thank you. At the time I would like to introduce Congressman Holt. You are recognized to introduce Ms. Bean.

Continue....

Mr. Mitchell. Mr. Cintron, in your testimony you say that the VA's suicide prevention hotline and suicide prevention efforts aren't working. Can you please elaborate on why you think that?

Mr. Cintron. Yes, sir. I believe, Mr. Chairman, that--and I am an aviation safety professional. I have a responsibility for safety. The things that we try to do is never go to an accident site but rather prevent the accident from happening. But the suicide hotline the way it is, and you are either don't have a problem serious enough to consider and you can wait and make a appointment 3, 4 weeks down the road, or you are suicidal.

There is no intervention in between. There is no prevention. There is no strategy there to say how do we keep our soldiers and our veterans from getting to that stage.

I am very glad that the hotline is there. Please don't misunderstand. I think it is needed. However, by not having something in the program that allows somebody to just talk or just keep them from going to the next level, because they don't have an outlet, that now they will get there, and by the time they reach the suicide hotline it is too late. We could have prevented them from even getting there.

The numbers that you stated today are stunning to me, both in the soldiers that we are losing, the veterans that we are losing, and in the good way, the ones that we are preventing. But I say we could prevent so many more if there was a prevention strategy of keeping them from getting to a suicide hotline.

One of the things that I would like to say, Mr. Chairman, is that programs such as are out there for our folks to interact with, are critical. But it also has to be part of the military's program. And I will share this example with you.

When I came out of Iraq the second time around, we were in Fort Dix being outprocessed. As we are being given all our out briefings, a sergeant steps up and says who here needs to talk to somebody for anything you have seen or done? And nobody raised their hand. Nobody said here. He said okay, if you want to do it confidentially, we will have a board, a tablet that you can sign up on. The day before we left Fort Dix, same sergeant stood in an auditorium with that board and read those names and said, do you still need to talk to somebody?

I was one of those soldiers. I did not need to talk to somebody at that time.

So there has to be an interlacing, collaborative effort to also get the services involved in having peer-to-peer training in identifying, you know we have the buddy system, we have the life saver program for a soldier that doesn't have to be a trained medic to be able to provide that first aid lifesaving technique. They have that. We can have the same thing, but we are talking about saving a soldier's mind and saving their life.

www.ingramcontent.com/pod-product-compliance
Lightning Source LLC
Chambersburg PA
CBHW051311120626
46547CB00015B/2186